FLORIDA SEAFOOD COOKERY

Tasty and Economical Recipes for the Preparation of Fish, Crabs, Oysters, Shrimp, Clams, Crawfish Scallops and Sea Turtles

Compiled by Editors

FEDERAL WRITERS' PROJECT
Florida, June, 1943

Creative Cookbooks
Monterey, California

Florida Seafood Cookery

Compiled by
Federal Writers' Project

ISBN: 1-4101-0666-7

Copyright © 2004 by Fredonia Books

Reprinted from the 1945 edition

Creative Cookbooks
An Imprint of Fredonia Books
Monterey, California
http://www.creativecookbooks.com

CONTENTS

TABLE OF WEIGHTS AND MEASURES

3 teaspoons ....1 tablespoon
16 tablespoons ....1 cup
2 cups ....1 pint
4 cups of liquid ....1 quart
4 cups of flour ....1 quart
2 cups of solid butter ....1 pound
2 cups granulated sugar ....1 pound
2½ cups powdered sugar ....1 pound
2 cups milk or water ....1 pound
1 tablespoon butter.............................1 ounce

Oven Temperature

Slow ....250°-300°
Moderate ....300°-375°
Hot ....375°-425°
Very Hot ....425°-500°

Abbreviations Used in Book

Tbsp. ....Tablespoon
Tsp. ....Teaspoon
Lb. ....Pound
Pt. ....Pint
Qt. ....Quart

iv

PURCHASING OF FISH AND SHELLFISH

For the economical purchase of fish and shellfish, the homemaker, in addition to personal preference, should give consideration to those in season; whether the food to be purchased is desired for baking, frying, or boiling; and to the purchase of first class material.

Fish and shellfish, like many other types of food products, have a time during the year when they are in season. Some varieties are available only a few months in the year, others the year around. Progressive seafood merchants are

WHOLE or ROUND FISH -   Fish as landed.

DRAWN FISH -   Entrails only are removed.

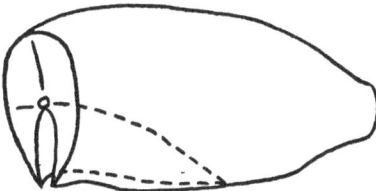

DRESSED FISH -   Entrails, head and tail, and usually fins are removed.

always glad to advise the varieties in season, and also the best ways to cook them.

Because of the delicate structure of fish and shellfish, these foods will spoil easily if not handled with care. For this reason they must be well iced and also protected from contamination.

Freshness in fish is detected by the color of the gills; light red, denotes freshness; dark red, staleness. The flesh should be firm, and if a whole fish is purchased, see that the eyes are bright and not sunken, that the scales cling to the skin, and above all, that there is no odor of taint.

Fresh fish and shellfish should be kept cool—preferably wrapped in parchment paper—and placed in a refrigerator until cooking is started.

When oysters and clams are bought in the shell, it is important that the shells be firmly held together, since this shows they are alive. Shucked oysters, clams, and scallops, when properly handled, will keep fresh for relatively long periods. Unless crabs and lobsters have been cooked previous to marketing, they should be alive when sold at retail.

Frozen fish, if properly handled, will remain in perfect condition for months. Frozen fish fillets may be placed immediately in the cooking utensil, but large fish, or thick slices of steaks and fillets should be defrosted by soaking in cold water.

Salt or smoked fish generally may be kept in cool air for several days without refrigeration. Canned fish (hermetically sealed) will keep indefinitely if stored in a cool, dry place.

Fillets, steaks, or pan-dressed fish are ready for cooking without further preparation. Fillets are the meaty sides cut lengthwise away from the backbone of fish, weighing from $1\frac{1}{2}$ to 4 pounds; the skin with the scales removed may be left on one side of the fillet. Steaks are cut crosswise from larger fish, after scaling and skinning, and have a thickness of $\frac{5}{8}$ inch or more. Pan-dressed fish are whole fish which have been scaled and freed from all traces of viscera and blood. The head, tail, and fins may be removed.

If more whole fish are purchased than are desired for immediate cooking, they may be preserved as corned fish for a few days by splitting along the backbone into slices not over $\frac{5}{8}$ inch in thickness, then covering all surfaces of each slice with fine salt, placing the fish in deep dish and storing for 6 to 12 hours in a refrigerator. Thus preserved, they may be cooked by boiling for 10 minutes, seasoned with butter, and pepper, and served with toast. If pickled for more than 12 hours, they should be freshened by soaking for a short time in cold water, then baked or broiled.

In general, fish should be served as soon as possible after cooking. Suddenly subjecting fish to the maximum temperature when frying, baking or broiling, tends to preserve the flavor, then reduce temperature to complete the process of cooking.

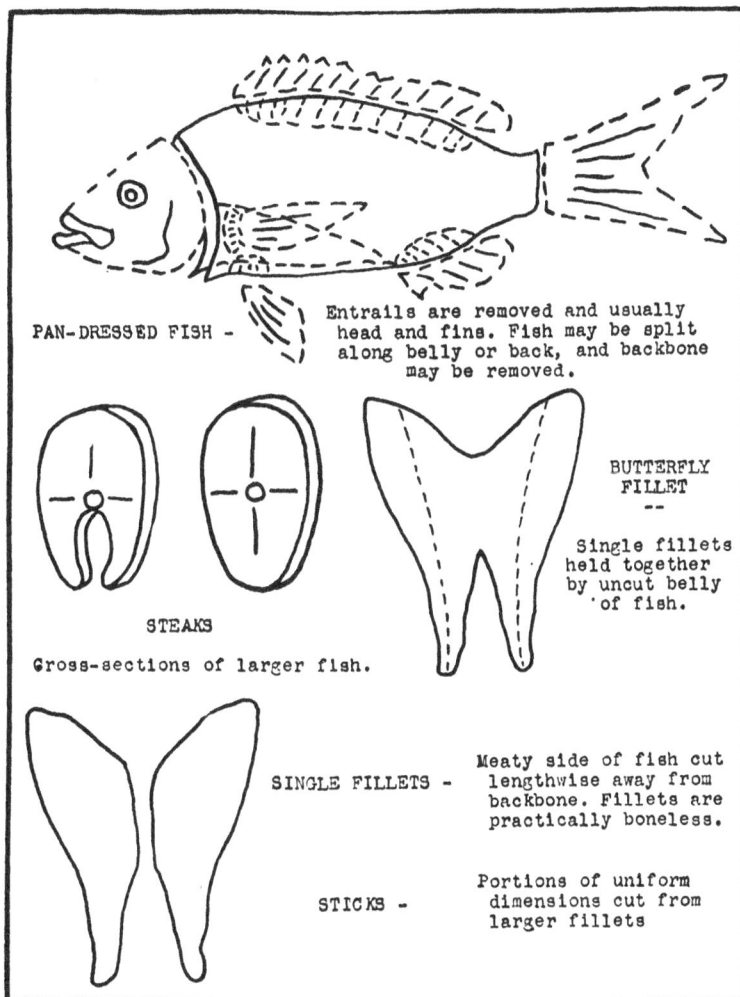

PAN-DRESSED FISH - Entrails are removed and usually head and fins. Fish may be split along belly or back, and backbone may be removed.

STEAKS

Cross-sections of larger fish.

BUTTERFLY FILLET
--
Single fillets held together by uncut belly of fish.

SINGLE FILLETS - Meaty side of fish cut lengthwise away from backbone. Fillets are practically boneless.

STICKS - Portions of uniform dimensions cut from larger fillets

Thoroughly chilling the hands, before handling fish, will prevent any odor clinging to them. Afterwards cleanse the hands by washing in hot water with salt, but no soap, until after rinsing off the salt. A strong, hot solution of salt in water (without soap) removes the odor of fish from dishes.

LEAN AND FAT FLORIDA FISHES

The fat content of fish varies according to species and to a lesser extent according to season. Almost any variety of fish may be fried or broiled, but fat fish are generally preferred for baking, while lean fish are ordinarily used for boiling, steaming, or chowders. Lean fish (cooked otherwise than frying) supply fewer calories than fat fish. While many enjoy fried fish, it is suggested that invalids be served fish which has been prepared by other methods than frying. It is especially suggested that fish for the evening meal be baked, broiled, steamed, or in chowder form.

Following is a list of the fishes classified as "lean" or "fat":

Lean	Season	Fat	Season
Bluefish	All year	Barracuda	Feb.-June
Blue Pike	Mar.-Dec.	Catfish	All year
Carp	Apr.-Dec.	Eels	All year
Crappie	All year	Mackerel (Spanish)	Nov.-May
Croker (hardhead)	All year	Pompano	All year
Drum	Nov.-June	Porgie	All year
Flounder	Nov.-June	Scup	All year
Grouper	Nov.-May	Shad	All year
Halibut	All year	Whitefish	Apr.-Dec.
Kingfish	Jan.-June		
King Whiting	All year		
Mullet (popeye)	All year		
Red Snapper	All year		
Sea Bass (black fish)	All year		
Sheepshead	All year		
Sunfish	Dec.-June		
Swordfish	June-Oct.		
Weakfish (sea trout)	Apr.-Nov.		
White Bass	All year		
Whiting (silver hake)	May-Dec.		
Yellow Perch	All year		

SAUCES FOR SEAFOODS

BROWN SAUCE (1)*
(6 Servings)

3 tbsp. butter
2 tbsp. flour
1 cup hot milk or stock
½ tsp. salt
¼ tsp. pepper

Method:

1 Brown the butter and flour in a saucepan.
2 Heat the milk; do not let it scorch.
3 Slowly pour in hot milk or meat stock while stirring.
4 Add seasoning and cook until smooth and thick; stir constantly.

* Note: The number in parenthesis after title refers to the source of the recipe which will be found under the head of "Citations" at the end of the book.

CAPER SAUCE (1)
(6 Servings)

2 tbsp. butter
¼ cup flour
½ tsp. salt
Cayenne pepper
1 ½ cups hot meat stock or fish
    liquid or boiling water
1 tsp. onion juice
½ cup capers

Method:
1 Melt butter.
2 Remove from heat and add flour.
3 When smooth add salt, pepper, stock and onion juice.
4 Stir until thick.
5 Add capers and serve.

CREOLE SAUCE (2)
(8 Servings)

4 tbsp. melted butter
½ cup minced onion
1 cup minced sweet pepper
1 clove garlic, minced
2 cups stewed or canned tomatoes
1 tsp. salt
¾ tsp. pepper
½ tsp. paprika

Method:
1 Simmer butter, onion, pepper, garlic in saucepan for 5 minutes.
2 Add the tomatoes and seasoning.
3 Boil for 5 minutes.
4 Serve hot.

Especially popular in the South, where it is used principally for baked fish.

Variations: The white meat of various kinds of seafood cut into slices not over ½-inch thick may be boiled in this sauce for about 10 minutes and served whole.

CUCUMBER SAUCE (1)
(6 Servings)

1 cup whipping cream
½ tsp. salt
⅛ tsp. cayenne
2 tbsp. vinegar
1 cucumber, chopped
¼ tsp. onion juice

Method:
1 Beat cream until until thick.
2 Add salt, cayenne.
3 Gradually add the vinegar.
4 Fold in cucumber and onion juice.
5 Serve very cold.

HOLLANDAISE SAUCE (1)
(6 Servings)

½ cup butter
3 beaten egg yolks
2 tbsp. lemon juice
½ tsp. salt
¼ tsp. pepper
½ cups boiling water

Method:
1 Cream the butter.
2 Add egg yolks; beat thoroughly.
3 Add lemon juice, salt, pepper, and boiling water.
4 Cook in double boiler until thick as custard.
5 Serve at once.

LEMON BUTTER (2)
(6 Servings)

4 tbsp. butter, melted
1 tsp. lemon juice
½ tsp. pepper

Method:
1 Blend.
2 Serve hot.

MAITRE D'HOTEL BUTTER (2)
(6 Servings)

½ cup butter (sold)
1 tbsp. lemon juice
1 tsp. minced parsley
⅛ tsp. pepper
⅛ tsp. salt

Method:
1 Cream the butter, gradually add the lemon juice, salt, and pepper.
2 When well blended, add parsley.
3 With butter paddles roll into balls about ¾-inch in diameter.
4 Chill. Place one butter ball at the side of each serving of fish.

Suggestion: A cold dressing often served with broiled or fried fish.

SPANISH SAUCE (1)
(6 Servings)

2 large green peppers, chopped
1 clove garlic, chopped
1 large onion, chopped
4 tbsp. bacon fat
4 cups canned tomatoes
1 tbsp. Worchestershire sauce
1 tsp. dry mustard
dash Cayenne
1½ tsp. salt

Method:
1 Cook peppers, garlic, and onion in bacon fat until brown.
2 Add tomatoes and seasoning.
3 Cook slowly for about 20 minutes until thick.

Suggestion: A can of mushrooms adds to flavor.

TARTAR SAUCE (2)
(6 Servings)

1 cup mayonnaise
1 tbsp. mixed pickles
1 tbsp. minced parsley
1 tbsp. mixed capers
1 tbsp. minced onion

Method:
1 Mix ingredients thoroughly.
2 Serve cold.

Suggestion: For serving with deep fried fish, oysters, scallops, etc.

TOMATO SAUCE (1)
(6 Servings)

2 cups canned tomatoes
2 tbsp. butter
2 tbsp. flour
1 tsp. Worcestershire sauce
½ tsp. salt
¼ tsp. pepper

Method:
1 Cook tomatoes 10 minutes.
2 Strain.
3 Melt butter.
4 Stir in flour.
5 Add hot tomato juice and seasoning.
6 Cook until it thickens.

CREAM OR WHITE SAUCE (2)
(6 Servings)

2 tbsp. butter
2 tbsp. white flour
1 cup milk heated
½ tsp. salt
¼ tsp. pepper

Method:
1 Heat butter in saucepan until it begins to bubble.
2 Stir in flour.
3 Add seasoning, and stir until whole is blended.
4 Gradually add the heated milk with continued stirring until smooth.
5 Serve hot.

Suggestion: This sauce may be used in creaming seafoods; chopped hard boiled eggs, mushrooms, capers, parsley, or onion give variety.

FISH

General Cooking Directions

The many ways in which fish may be prepared and served makes it possible for the homemaker to have it frequently on her menu for the week without the family appetite becoming jaded.

There are two methods of frying—saute or pan-frying and deep-fat frying. To pan-fry, the fish is cooked in a small amount of oil or fat, never butter, since it smokes at a relatively low temperature. In deep-fat frying, the fish is cooked

Preparing the Filets for Frying

in hot fat to cover, either by the basket-frying equipment, or in a deep pan. Steaks or fillets about ½ inch thick, or small fish of equal thickness are preferred. With thicker fish, there is danger of burning the outside before the inside is cooked.

Some cooks prefer to remove the skin from fat fish before frying. Plunge fish in boiling water, letting it remain for about half a minute. Lift into a plate or place on a fish board and remove the skin while the fish is hot.

Any clean fat or oil may be used for frying. Vegetable fats smoke at temperatures higher than do animal fats, and for this reason are preferred by many for home cooking.

The fish is cut into portions and dipped in some liquid—beaten egg, plain, or mixed with water; milk, or water, then covered with some dry ingredient such as corn meal, flour, cracker or bread crumbs, and seasoned. In tests at the laboratory of the U. S. Bureau of Fisheries, the most satisfactory method was to dip the fish into water and then to roll it in a well-prepared mixture of ½ cup fine unbolted yellow corn meal, ½ cup flour, and 1½ tsp. salt.

Heat the fat over a slow fire in a heavy cast-iron frying pan. Cut the fish into service portions, dip into water, then into dry ingredients. When the fat is hot, place the fish in the pan and cook 3 minutes. Cover the pan, remove from flame, and allow the fish to cook in its own steam about two minutes. Remove cover, turn fish, return pan to fire and cook three minutes longer.

Deep-fat Frying: Cut the fish into service portions, wet with water, and cover with the dry ingredients sifted together. Heat fat in a deep kettle provided with a frying basket, to a temperature of 385° to 400° F. (A piece of bread will brown in 20 to 25 seconds at this heat.) Put one layer of fish in the basket and cook to a golden brown. This will take from 3 to 8 minutes, depending upon the variety of fish. Do not attempt to fry more than one layer of fish at a time.

To Broil: This popular method of cooking may be used for many kinds of seafood. The method of seasoning is superior to older practices. Select for broiling:

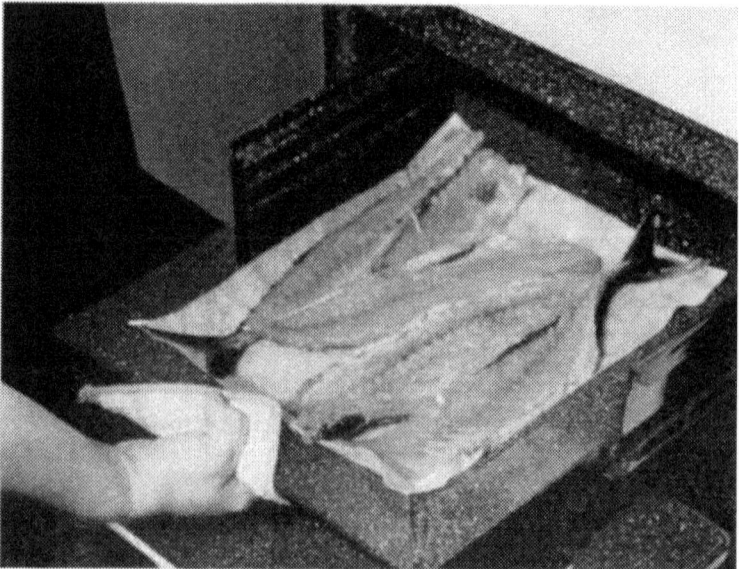

Fish in pan ready for broiling

	Method:
2 lbs. fillet steaks about ½-inch thick, or 3 lbs. whole fish, split	1 Dip fish in salt solution—2 tbsp. salt to 1 cup cold water (allow to stand 3 minutes). 2 Oil the preheated broiler pan. 3 Place fish about 2 inches below the heat (skin side up). 4 Cook until surface is brown. 5 Turn fish to brown other side. 6 Baste 3 times with melted butter or cooking oil. 7 Broil about 20 minutes.

Another method of broiling is to remove rack from broiler pan, placing a piece of waterproof paper in the pan. Dry fish, sprinkle with salt and pepper, brush with oil or fat. Place on paper in the broiler, flesh side up. Small fish are usually broiled whole with the heads left on. Larger fish are usually broiled when split down the back, then spread open. Slices or steaks are browned on one side, then on the other.

To Boil: Fish is usually boiled in court bouillon, a special preparation used by chefs for cooking fish. Homemakers generally use fish steak. This is water seasoned to taste with salt and vinegar, or lemon juice added. To give flavor, add vegetable seasonings—onions, carrots, bay leaf, or peppercorns. A 3-pound piece of fish should cook in 30 minutes. Remove skin from fish before serving. Serve with any desired sauce.

To Steam: Place fish on an oiled dish. Sprinkle with lemon juice and salt. Cover with waxed paper or cooking paper. Then place in steamer and steam until tender.

To Bake: (Whole) Either fat or lean fish may be used. The former is preferred by many, as they require less care. Lean fish should be slashed through the skin in several places, since there is less shrinkage of the flesh. Remove backbone. Sauces may be served with the fish as desired.

BAKED FISH (2)
(6 Servings)

	Method:
4-lb. fish, cleaned and trimmed but not split 4 strips of bacon Cooking oil Salt Stuffing: (or dressing) ¾ tsp. salt ¾ tsp. pepper 4 tbsp. hot celery liquid 4 tbsp. melted butter ¾ cup cooked celery, finely chopped 1 qt. bread crumbs 2 tbsp. finely crushed sage leaves 3 tbsp. finely chopped onion ½ cup hot milk or water	1 Dip fish into salt solution (2 tbsp. salt to 1 cup cold water). 2 Allow to stand 5 minutes. 3 Drain fish. 4 Slit the skin in several places. 5 Brush over with cooking oil. 6 Lay 2 strips of bacon in the greased baking pan. 7 Stuff the fish. 8 Tie with string to hold the stuffing. 9 Place it on the strips of bacon. 10 Lay strips of bacon on top of fish. 11 Bake for 10 minutes at 500° F. then 30 minutes at 400° F.

Another easy method is to take the whole fish, rub with salt inside and out. Stuff with dressing, if desired, and tie together. Place a piece of waxed paper or cooking paper in baking pan before putting in fish. Usual cooking time is 10 minutes per pound up to 4 pounds, then 5 minutes per pound.

BAKING FILLETS, STEAKS, OR SMALL FISH (2)
(6 Servings)

Method:

2 lbs. steaks or fillets about ¼-inch thick or about 3 whole fish dressed
1 cup bread crumbs
¼ tsp. pepper
2 tsp. grated onion
cooking oil

1 Preheat the oven to 500° F.
2 Cut the fish into serving portions.
3 Mix the pepper thoroughly into the bread crumbs.
4 Dip fish into a salt solution (2 tbsp. salt in 1 cup water).
5 Drain, roll in crumbs and pepper mixture.
6 Place on a greased baking dish.
7 Sprinkle with grated onion and cooking oil.
8 Bake near the top of oven for 15 to 20 minutes, depending upon the thickness and species of fish.

This method may be used for boneless fish, as well as fish too small for stuffing. Sauces may be served as desired.

SPENCER HOT OVEN BAKING (2)
(6 Servings)

Method:

2 lbs. of fillets or steaks
1 tbsp. salt
1 cup milk
Finely sifted bread crumbs
1 cup cooking oil or melted fat

1 Cut fish, 3 portions to 1 lb.
2 Mix salt and milk in a bowl.
3 Place bread crumbs in another bowl.
4 With a fork dip fish in milk.
5 Use dry fork, toss fish in crumbs.
6 Place in oiled banking pan.
7 Sprinkle with fat or oil.
8 Bake 10 minutes in 550° oven.
9 Remove to hot platter when golden brown on all sides.

Suggestion: Thin strips of bacon instead of oil or fat.

Permit

BOILED FISH IN PARCHMENT PAPER (2)
(6 Servings)

2 large sheets of parchment paper
2 lbs. absolutely boneless fillets
  Salt solution (2 tbsp. salt to
  1 cup water)
2 tbsp. butter or cooking oil
¼ tsp. pepper
2 tbsp. carrot (grated)
2 tbsp. onion (grated)
1 tbsp. parsley (chopped)
1 tbsp. lemon juice

Method:

1 Oil or wet both sides of parchment.
2 Let fish stand 5 minutes in salt solution.
3 Cut into servings.
4 Arrange on parchment, one layer deep only.
5 Mix butter and pepper.
6 Spread fish with 1 tsp. each butter, carrot, onion.
7 Sprinkle with lemon juice and parsley.
8 Bring edges of paper together and tie.
9 Place in kettle of boiling water.
10 Boil 20 minutes.
11 Remove to hot platter.
12 Pour juices over fish or thicken for gravy.

Suggestion: Same directions may be followed using steamer. Cook 25 minutes.

PLANKED FISH (2)
(6 Servings)

Oak plank with grooves
2 lbs. fillets ½ inch thick
  Salt solution (2 tbsp. salt to 1 cup water)
1 tbsp. grated onion
4 tbsp. butter
¼ tsp. pepper

Method:

1 Place plank in cold oven; heat to 450°.
2 Soak fish 3 minutes in salt solution.
3 Drain.
4 Brush with cooking oil.
5 Remove plank from oven, oil thoroughly, and place fish on plank, skin side down.
6 Sprinkle with grated onion, and return to top rack in the oven.
7 Cook 20 minutes, basting once or twice with butter-pepper dressing.

Suggestion: About five minutes before fish is cooked, it may be surrounded with mashed potatoes and cooked vegetables, as desired.

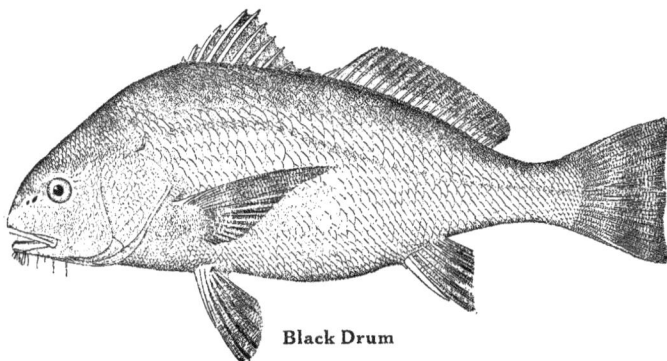

Black Drum

FISH CHOWDERS (2)
(6 Servings)

This "complete-meal", popular for generations in certain parts of the country, is worthy of trial by those to whom it may be new. Almost any white-meated lean fish is suitable for chowders.

½ cup salt pork, diced
¼ cup sliced onions
3 cups sliced potatoes
1 tsp. salt
¼ tsp. pepper
1 cup water
2 lbs. lean fish

Method:

1 In heavy kettle, fry pork to a golden brown color.
2 Add onions and fry these to a light yellow color.
3 Add the potatoes, sprinkle with salt and pepper.
4 Add cup of water.
5 Cook until potatoes are about half done.
6 Add fish, flesh side down.
7 Cook until potatoes are soft.
8 Remove any skin from the fish and break the flesh into coarse flakes.
9 Serve hot.

FORT GEORGE ISLAND FISH CHOWDER (3)
(18 Servings)

6 medium sized potatoes
6 onions (small)
6 lbs. whole fish (fat) with plenty of meat
6 slices breakfast bacon
¼ tsp. pepper
½ tsp. salt
1 can evaporated milk
Tabasco sauce

Method:

1 Dice potatoes.
2 Chop onions.
3 Boil separately, use small amount of water.
4 Clean fish.
5 Cook in small amount of water.
6 Discard skin and bones.
7 Reserve all liquid.
8 Invert dinner plate in bottom of iron pot.
9 Cover with thin slices of breakfast bacon.
10 Combine potatoes, onions, fish and liquids and pour into iron pot.
11 Add 1 can evaporated milk.
12 Season with salt and pepper, and tabasco.
13 Cook 30 minutes.

Suggestion: This is a good dish for family picnics or parties at the beach, and may be prepared on an out-of-door camp fire.

FISH WITH VEGETABLES (2)
(6 Servings)

3 lbs. cabbage (waste removed)
Salt
2 lbs. fillets or steaks of fish
Cooking oil

Basting Mixture:
4 tbsp. melted butter
¼ tsp. black pepper
4 tbsp. garlic, green pepper, or
onion vinegar

Method:

1 Quarter cabbage.
2 Soak in salt water 10 minutes.
3 Cut in coarse shreds in salted water.
4 Boil in uncovered kettle.
5 Place fish in salt solution for 3 minutes.
6 Drain fish.
7 Brush on both sides with oil.
8 Hang fish in steamer or basket over cabbage.
9 Boil 5 minutes.
10 Spread cabbage on oiled plank.
11 Lay fish, skin down, on cabbage.
12 Baste with butter mixture.
13 Broil until brown.

Variation: Very appetizing one-dish meals may be prepared by combining fish with approximately equal quantities of vegetables—onions, cabbage, sauerkraut, snap (string) beans, or apples.

BOILED FISH AND VEGETABLE DINNER (2)
(6 Servings)

¼ cup diced salt pork (fat back)
2 cups water
½ lb. each turnips, potatoes, onions and carrots
1 lb. cabbage
1 tsp. salt
½ tsp. pepper
2 lbs. fillets, steaks, or pan-dressed fish

Method:

1 In a heavy kettle, fry the pork to a golden brown.
2 Add 1 cup water, and all the vegetables except the cabbage, which is cooked separately.
3 Allow vegetables to cook 20 minutes.
4 Add salt, pepper and second cup of water.
5 Lay the fish, flesh side down, across the vegetables.
6 Cover with cabbage.
7 Cook the whole about 5 minutes more.
8 Place the fish in the center of a large platter, surrounded by the vegetables.
9 The liquid remaining in the kettle may be served in a side bowl.

FISH AND APPLES (2)
(6 Servings)

2 lbs. fillets or steaks, about ½ inch thick
3 tbsp. butter or cooking fat
2½ lbs. apples (9 of medium size)
½ tsp. salt
1 tsp. sugar
Basting oil
4 tbsp. melted butter
¼ tsp. black pepper

Method:

1 Cover fish with a salt solution (2 tbsp. salt to 1 cup water) for 3 minutes and drain.
2 Heat fat slowly in a deep frying pan.
3 Slice apples ¼ inch thick.
4 Place the apples in the hot fat, add the water, salt and sugar.
5 Cover and cook slowly until almost tender.
6 Lay the fish, flesh side down, on the apples, cover and allow to steam 5 minutes.
7 Remove cover, turn the fish and baste with the butter and pepper.
8 Place for 15 minutes under broiler until well browned.
9 Remove the fish to a hot platter and surround with the apples.

FILLET A LA POULETTE (4)
(Sarasota)
(6 Servings)

2 lbs. fish fillets
Salt and pepper
Juice of one lemon
2 onions, sliced
1/3 cup melted butter
2 cups sauce

Method:

1 Wipe the fillets with a damp cloth.
2 Season with salt and pepper.
3 Sprinkle with lemon juice and place in deep pan.
4 Cover with sliced onion.
5 Let stand 30 minutes.
6 Dip fillets in melted butter, then in flour.
7 Arrange in greased baking dish, cover with onion and bake 25 minutes in oven heated to 400° F.

Sauce

2 tbsp. butter
2 tbsp. flour
2 cups rich milk
Salt and pepper
Worcestershire sauce
Lemon, or lime, or sprigs cress

Method:

1 Melt butter in saucepan.
2 Add flour.
3 When blended add milk.
4 Stir until smooth and thick.
5 Season to taste with salt, pepper, and few drops Worcestershire sauce.
6 Keep over hot water until needed.
7 Lift fillets to heated platter, garnish with lemon or lime wedges, or springs of cress.
8 Serve with sauce piping hot.

Variation: Two hard-boiled eggs, sliced, or ½ cup grated cheese may be added.

FILLET FISH WITH PARMESAN (4)
(Sarasota)
(6 Servings)

1 cup grated Parmesan cheese
2 egg yolks
6 fillets
Salt, pepper, and cayenne
2 tbsp. butter
2 tbsp. flour
1 cup milk
1 tbsp. lemon juice
1 tbsp. thick cream

Method:

1 Mix half the cheese with egg yolks, dash cayenne, salt.
2 Spread the mixture inside the fillets.
3 Lay the fillets on a buttered pan, cover with paper.
4 Bake in moderate oven 15 minutes.

Sauce
1 Melt the butter in a saucepan.
2 Stir in the flour.
3 Add the milk, stirring constantly.
4 Cook for 5 minutes.
5 Add the cream, lemon, salt and pepper.
6 Remove paper.
7 Place the fillets in a circle in a baking dish.
8 Pour the sauce over the fish.
9 Sprinkle with remainder of cheese.
10 Bake in a moderate oven until brown on top.

FISH TURBAN (4)
(Sarasota)
(6 Servings)

3 lb. fish
Rich cream sauce
2 egg yolks, beaten
Cracker crumbs

Method:

1 Wrap a 3 lb. fish in cheesecloth.
2 Steam or boil 25 minutes.
3 When cool, flake and remove skin and bones.
4 Make a rich thick cream sauce. (See p. 10).
5 Add the beaten yolks of 2 eggs.
6 Pile in pyramid form, first a layer of fish, then a layer of sauce, covering the top with buttered cracker crumbs.
7 Bake in oven until slightly brown.
8 Serve hot.

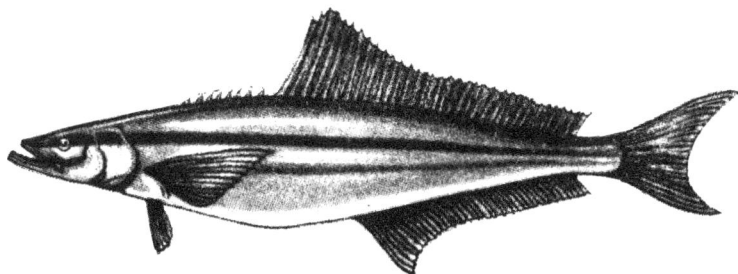

Cobia

KEDGREE (4)
(Sarasota)
(4 Servings)

2 tbsp. butter
½ lb. cold flaked fish
1 cup boiled rice
2 eggs, hard boiled
Salt and pepper
Parsley

Method:

1 Melt butter in pan.
2 Stir in fish, rice, chopped eggs, and seasoning.
3 Stir until heated thoroughly.
4 Pile high on a hot platter.
5 Garnish with parsley.
6 Sprinkle with a little chopped parsley.

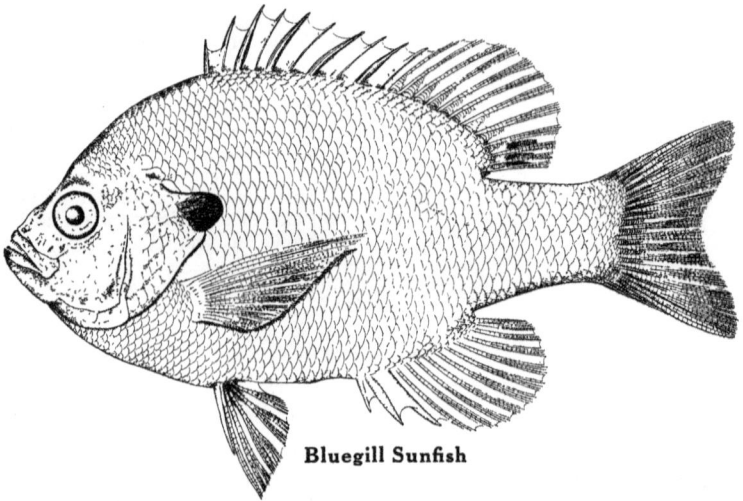

Bluegill Sunfish

FISH STEAKS (5)
(Hawaiian)
(6 Servings)

1 cup cooked rice
1 cup soft bread crumbs
1 small onion, minced
2 cups drained crushed pineapple
Salt and paprika
Fish steaks (6 servings)

Method:

1 Mix 1 cup cooked rice with 1 cup soft bread crumbs, 1 small onion, minced, and 2 cups drained pineapple.
2 Season with salt and paprika.
3 Put fish steaks in oiled baking dish.
4 Cover with mixture.
5 Cover with a second layer of steaks.
6 Pour pineapple juice in baking dish.
7 Bake in a hot oven until fish is cooked.

SPECIAL FLORIDA FISH RECIPES
BLUEFISH (5)
(6 to 8 Servings)

Bluefish are sold whole, their average weight from 3 to 6 pounds. Snapper blues or young fish, weigh less. The flesh is soft, and the fish is best when baked or broiled.

1 Bluefish
3 cups soft bread crumbs
1 small onion, minced
3 tbsp. butter
Salt

Method:

1 Rub the fish inside and out with salt.
2 Make the stuffing with 3 cups of soft bread crumbs, 1 small onion, minced and cook in 3 tbsp. butter until soft.
3 Pack into body cavity and sew up.
4 Bake in a hot oven 10 minutes per pound.

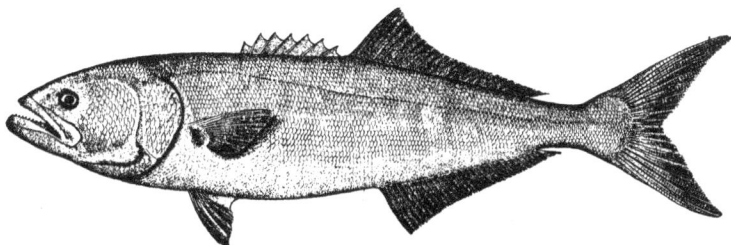

Bluefish

PORGIES (3)
(2 to 6 Servings)

Porgies, also called Scups, weigh ½ to 2 pounds, and are sold whole. They may be pan-fried, or broiled. Large fish should be split.

Fish
Cooking oil
Salt and pepper
Melted butter

To Broil:

1 Brush one side of fish with oil.
2 Season with salt and pepper.
3 Cook under medium flame in broiler until brown.
4 Turn fish, brush with oil, season and cook.
5 Brush fish with melted butter.
6 Serve hot.

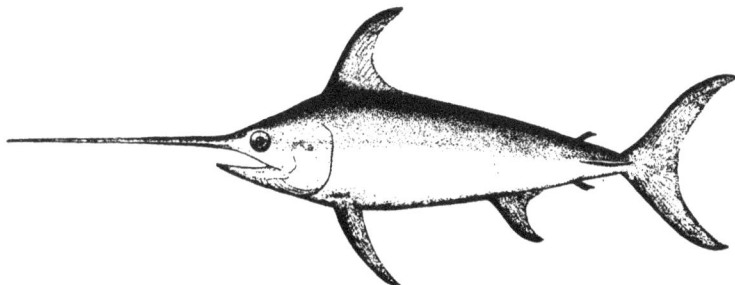

Swordfish

SEA BASS (5)
(2 to 6 Servings)

The sea bass has a white, flaky flesh, and weighs from 1 to 8 pounds. This fish responds to any cooking methods, and is good in chowders.

SEA BASS ANTIBES (5)
(6 Servings)

2 sea bass
2 tbsp. salted almonds
6 mushrooms
4 tbsp. butter or oil
1 tsp. chopped parsley
2 lemons

Method:
1 Place well-seasoned bass in oiled baking dish.
2 Chop almonds and mushrooms and mix with butter or oil, and parsley.
8 Spread this mixture over the fish.
4 Bake, basting several times.
5 Just before serving, pour juice of two lemons over fish.

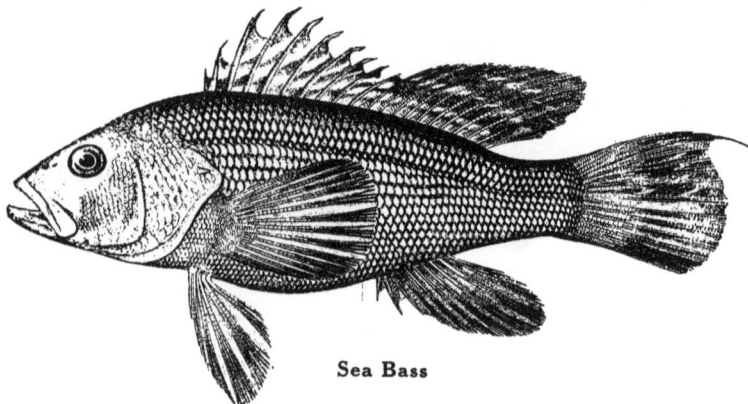

Sea Bass

SEA BASS CASTANO (5)
(6 Servings)

1 large sea bass
Salt and pepper
Dressing:
½ lb. mashed peanuts
5 tbsp. bread crumbs
½ tsp. chopped parsley
½ tsp. thyme
½ lemon, grated rind and juice
1 egg, beaten
Salt and pepper to taste

Method:
1 Season bass with salt and pepper.
2 Prepare dressing.
8 Stuff fish with dressing.
4 Place fish in baking pan.
5 Brush with oil.
6 Bake in hot oven until tender, about 30 minutes.

SHAD (5)
(2 to 8 Servings)

Shad is distinguished by its silvery color and dark spots. It is soft-fleshed, fat and bony. Sold whole, the average weight ranges from 1½ to 6 pounds. Roe shad is female with roe and commands the highest price. Cut shad is female with roe removed, and buck is male shad. Roe is sold separately. Shad is sauted, boiled, broiled, and baked.

BAKED SHAD (5)
(2 to 8 Servings)

1 Shad
Bread dressing
Strips of bacon or salt pork
1 tbsp. catsup
1 tbsp. flour
Juice of 1 lemon
1 small glass of grape or current
jelly

Method:

1 Stuff shad with bread dressing and place in baking dish.
2 Spread fish with oil, or lay strips of bacon or salt pork over it.
3 Put a small amount of water in baking pan.
4 Bake 30 minutes for 3 lb. fish; 45 to 60 minutes for larger fish.
5 Remove fish.
6 Add to liquid in pan catsup, flour, lemon juice and jelly.
7 Boil up, strain, and pour over fish.

SHAD SULTANA (5)
(6 Servings)

1 shad
½ cup water
Juice of 1 lemon
1 or 2 fresh tomatoes, or
1 can drained tomatoes, or
Parsley, chopped
½ cup raisins
Salt and pepper
Butter or cooking oil

Method:

1 Split the fish as for broiling.
2 Lay flesh side up on an oiled baking pan.
3 Pour ½ cup water, mixed with juice of lemon over fish.
4 Cover with tomato slices, or drained canned tomatoes.
5 Sprinkle with chopped parsley.
6 Scatter raisins over fish.
7 Season with salt and pepper.
8 Dot fish liberally with butter, or pour cooking oil over the top.
9 Bake 30 minutes at 400° F.

SHAD DE LUXE (5)
(6 Servings)

1 onion
1 shad
3 cups water
Salt
6 peppercorns
1 small stick cinnamon
2 lemons, sliced
1 tbsp. sugar
1 large apple, sliced
12 almonds, chopped
¼ cup raisins
2 eggs, beaten
1 tbsp. cornstarch

Method:

1 Cook onion in water 5 minutes.
2 Add shad, seasoned with salt, peppercorns, and cinnamon.
3 Cook 10 minutes.
4 Add lemons, sliced, seeds removed, sugar, apple, almonds, and raisins.
5 Cook until fish is done, about 10 minutes.
6 Remove fish.
7 Thicken stock by adding eggs and 1 tbsp. cornstarch, mixed with a little water.
8 Cook 1 minute.
9 Pour sauce over fish.

STRIPED BASS (5)
(3 to 10 Servings)

Striped bass is a soft-fleshed fish, sometimes called rockfish, averaging 2 to 5 pounds in weight. It is best when broiled.

1 striped bass
oil or fat
Salt and pepper
1 cup mayonnaise
1 tsp. capers, chopped
Parsley
Sweet pickle
3 tbsp. tomato catsup

Method:
1 Split the fish.
2 Brush flesh side with oil or fat.
3 Season with salt and pepper.
4 Broil 20 minutes.
5 Mix mayonnaise with capers, parsley, sweet pickle, and catsup.
6 Pour over fish.

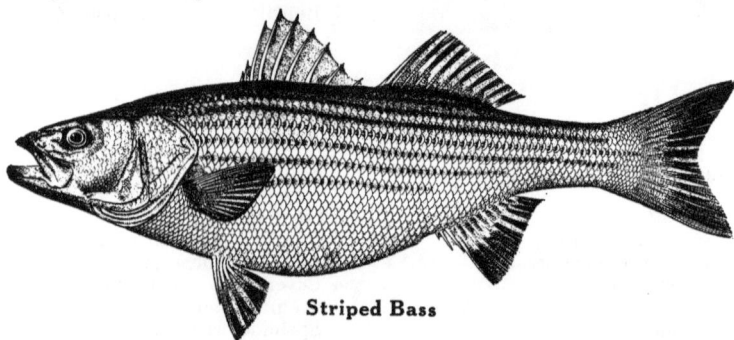

Striped Bass

SEA TROUT OR WEAKFISH (5)
(3 to 10 Servings, According to Size)

The flesh is lean and flaky. Fish weigh up to 5 pounds and are sold whole. Adaptable to any form of cooking.

1 small weakfish
Salt and pepper
Mayonnaise that has a good oil base

Method:
1 Season weakfish with salt and pepper.
2 Spread one side liberally with mayonnaise.
3 Place oiled side down on hot frying pan.
4 Cook until brown.
5 Spread other side with mayonnaise.
6 When it is brown, serve.

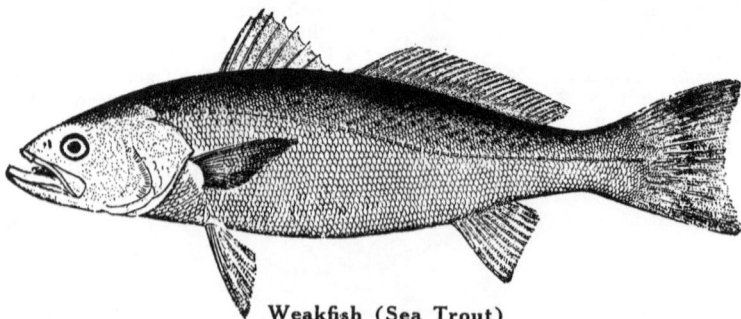

Weakfish (Sea Trout)

SPECKLED TROUT, CHEF'S STYLE (6)
(10 Servings)

1 5-lb. trout
Flour
Butter
Shrimp
Eggplant, diced
Onions, green
Parsley
Lemon juice
Lea & Perrin's Sauce

Method:

1 Cut trout tenderloins in strips like French fried potatoes.
2 Season and roll in flour.
3 Saute in butter with shrimp.
4 Smother diced eggplant in butter till tender.
5 Make a brown butter sauce with chopped green onions and parsley, lemon juice, and dash of Lea and Perrin's sauce.
6 Put trout and shrimp on platter, spread eggplant on top.
7 Pour butter sauce over the whole.

KING MACKEREL

King mackerel is also called kingfish. Weighs usually 5 to 7 pounds and is sold whole or sliced. It is distinguished from other mackerel by weight, by its bluer tint, silvery belly, and dark horizontal streak. Recipes for bluefish and mackerel may be applied to kingfish.

Kingfish

SAUTED KING MACKEREL (5)
(6 Servings)

2 lbs. of kingfish, sliced
Milk
Flour, or
Corn meal
Cooking oil or fat
Salt and pepper
Lemon

Method:

1 Dip slices of fish in salted milk.
2 Roll in seasoned flour or corn meal.
3 Heat a liberal amount of oil or fat in iron frying pan.
4 Brown the steaks on one side.
5 Turn, brown on the other.
6 Serve with a quarter of lemon.

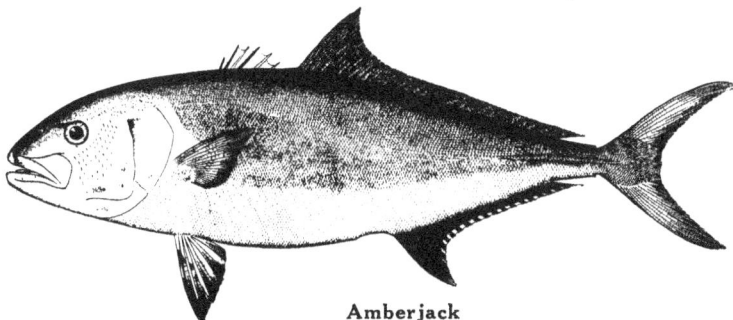

Amberjack

BAKED KING OR SPANISH MACKEREL (6)
(6 Servings)
Fillets weighing 9 to 12 oz. each, and up.

Method:

6 fillets
Olive oil
Salt
Butter
Paprika
Milk

1 Brush the fish lightly with olive oil.
2 Sprinkle well with salt.
3 Place portions close together in a well buttered pan.
4 Sprinkle cut portions with paprika.
5 Pour hot milk in the pan to the depth of ½ inch.
6 Place in oven heated to 350° F. and bake until the fish is browned on top.
7 Baste 3 to 4 times during the baking.

SPANISH MACKEREL (5)

Spanish mackerel has a slender bluish body, with 3 to 4 lines of oval bronze spots running from head to tail. They weigh from 1 to 3 pounds and are sold as whole fish. Best when broiled or sauted.

Spanish Mackerel

BROILED SPANISH MACKEREL (5)
(6 Servings)

Method:

1 3-lb. Spanish Mackerel
Salt and pepper
Cooking oil or fat
Melted butter
Paprika

1 Split fish.
2 Place on rack, skin side up, if skin has not been removed.
3 Broil at 450° F. until skin browns.
4 Turn.
5 Spread with butter, sprinkle with salt and paprika.
6 When brown, remove from pan.
7 Serve with lemon.

MULLET

Mullet, known as Florida's "money fish," are caught in large quantities in Florida, particularly along the Gulf coast, and are good the year round. They range in size from 1 to 3 pounds, and are sold whole or filleted.

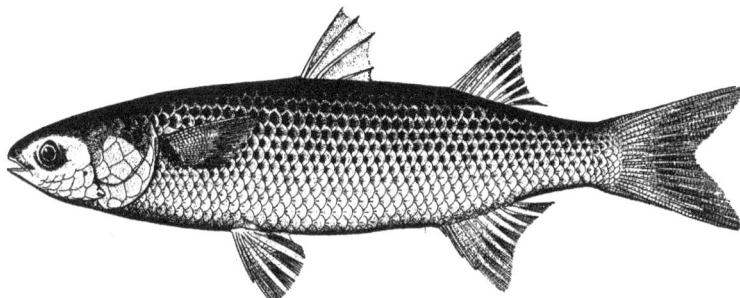

Mullet

FRIED MULLET SOUTHERN STYLE (5)
(6 Servings)

Method:

4 pounds of mullet
Salt and pepper
1 egg, slightly beaten
Corn meal
Fat

1 Clean and wash the fish.
2 Dry on clean towel.
3 Season with salt and pepper.
4 Dip into slightly beaten egg.
5 Roll in corn meal.
6 Fry in deep fat.
7 Drain on crushed paper.

MULLET BAKED IN CLAY (7)
(6 Servings)

Method:

1 4-lb. mullet
Leaves
Clay
Seasoning

1 Wrap dressed mullet in leaves.
2 Roll in soft clay.
3 Bake in open fire or glowing coals.
4 When the clay is burned hard, break with a hammer and open carefully. The mullet skin will adhere to the leaves, and the fish may be removed intact.

A Florida dish, popular with picnic or fishing parties.

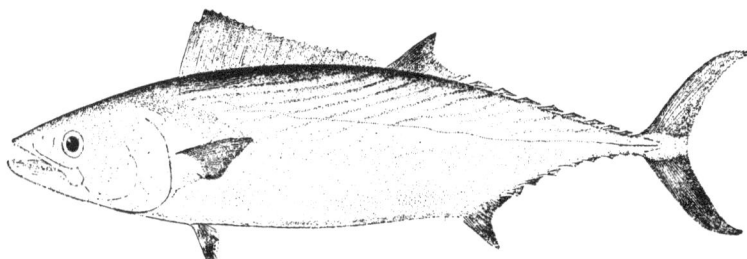

Bonito

POMPANO (5)
(6 Servings)

Pompano is considered Florida's "fish de luxe" and commands the highest price. The fish is delicate and especially fine-flavored.

1 4-lb. pompano
Salt and pepper
Lemon
Parsley

Method:

To Broil:
1 Split pompano down the back.
2 Wash and wipe dry.
3 Sprinkle with salt and pepper.
4 Place on a well greased wire broiler in 450° oven, skin side up.
5 Cook until skin browns.
6 Turn and brown on flesh side.
7 Broil 20 minutes.
8 Slip onto a hot platter and garnish with lemon and parsley.

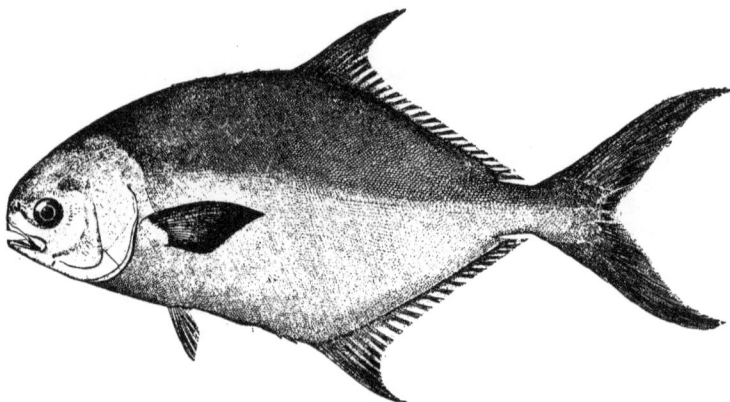

Pompano

BAKED POMPANO SUPREME (5)
(6 Servings)

2½ to 3-lb. pompano
Filling
Parsley
Julienne potatoes
Lemon

Filling:
1 cup croutons
1 cup peas
1 egg, beaten
2 tbsp. butter
1 small onion, chopped
3 stalks celery, chopped
Parsley, minced
½ tsp. salt
¼ tsp pepper

Method:
1 Clean and wipe fish dry.
2 Prepare the dressing by mixing the croutons, peas, beaten egg, butter, chopped onion, celery, and parsley, seasoned with salt and pepper.
3 Fill fish with dressing.
4 Bake 45 minutes at 400° F.
5 Serve, garnished with parsley, Julienne potatoes, lemon.

POMPANO PAPILLOTTE (6)

(4 Servings)

(Cook in Parchment Paper)

Method:

Stuffing:

5 fresh mushrooms
1 medium onion
2 tbsp. butter
2 tbsp. flour
½ pint fish stock
1 cup cream
1 cup crab meat
1 dozen cooked shrimp
1 2-lb. pompano

1 Chop mushrooms and onion.
2 Fry in butter until brown.
3 Add flour and mix well.
4 Add fish stock and cream and boil
  2 minutes.
5 Add crab meat, shrimp, and
  sherry.
6 Remove from heat.

To Bake Fish:

1 Roll pompano in flour.
2 Fry lightly in butter.
3 Fill with stuffing.
4 Lay on oil parchment.
5 Fold diagonally and twist edges
  together to make air tight.
6 Bake at 375 degrees for 15 minutes.
7 Serve in paper.

Suggestion: Lay two cooked shrimp and one whole boiled mushroom on top of fish, before enclosing in paper.

BAKED SPECKLED TROUT (5)

(6 Servings)

Method:

1 tbsp. butter
2 tbsp. parsley, finely chopped
Salt and pepper
¾ cup white wine
1 cup cooked mushrooms
1 4-lb. speckled trout
Juice of one-half lemon
Boston brown bread

1 Brown butter with parsley in a
  baking dish on surface unit of
  stove. Salt and pepper.
2 Add wine and mushrooms.
3 Place fish in baking dish and pour
  mixture over it.
4 Put in oven and bake, basting frequently.
5 When fish is cooked, pour liquid
  into a saucepan, boil it down well.
6 Stir in a second tsp. butter and
  pour it over the fish.
7 Squeeze the juice of lemon over
  fish.
8 Serve on hot platter with thin
  slices of Boston brown bread, well
  buttered.

RED SNAPPER

The Florida or Pensacola red snapper as it is commercially known, because that city is headquarters for the snapper fleet which produces nearly half the red snappers sold in the United States, is among the State's noted food fishes.

Snapper "jaws" (jowls), and throats, are the richest and most delicately flavored parts of the fish and may be purchased separate at the market. The small triangular pieces of flesh taken from the ventral side of the head are the throats; the jaws are taken farther back from the head. Both are used for chowder and salads, and can also be fried.

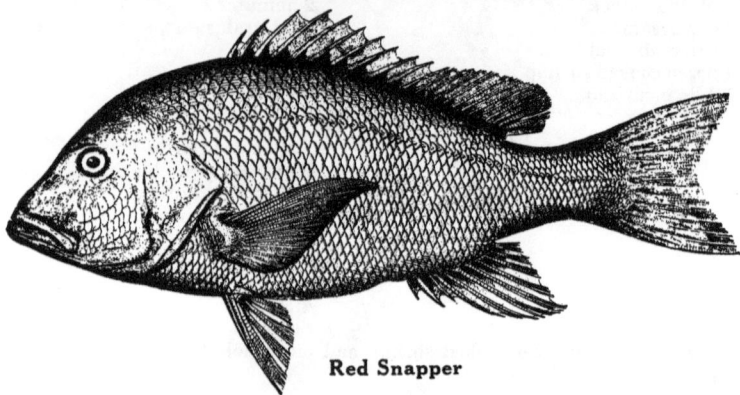

Red Snapper

SNAPPER CHOWDER

3 medium sized Irish potatoes, diced
3 lbs. red snapper
¾ cup diced salt pork, or bacon
3 medium sized onions, sliced
1 can tomatoes
1 green pepper, minced
1 cup chopped celery
1 can tomato paste
1 hot pepper
1 clove garlic

Method:

1 Boil potatoes until tender and save water.
2 Boil fish until tender, and save water.
3 Remove bones and skin, and break into small pieces.
4 Add water from fish and potatoes.
5 Fry bacon.
6 Remove from pan.
7 Saute the onion.
8 Add can of tomatoes, the pepper and celery.
9 Cook until tender.
10 Add tomato paste or can of tomato soup.
11 Put in large pot with fish.
12 Season and simmer.
13 Add the bacon and hot pepper, also garlic if desired.
14 Serve hot.

BAKED RED SNAPPER (1)
(3 lbs. 6 Servings)

Wash well and remove dark inside skin. Dry the fish, and stuff with the following:

3 lbs. red snapper
Salt and pepper
Butter
1 small onion
2 or 3 slices tomatoes
Bread crumbs

Dressing:
1 cup bread crumbs
4 tbsp. butter
1 tsp. onion juice
1 tsp. chopped parsley
1 tsp. lemon juice
½ tsp. salt
¼ tsp. pepper

Method:
1 Mix dressing.
2 Stuff fish
3 Place in a greased baking dish.
4 Season with salt and pepper, dot with butter.
5 Grate small onion over top of fish.
6 Lay on top two or three slices of tomatoes.
7 Sprinkle with a few bread crumbs.
8 Bake for 45 minutes at 350° F.

PRECOOKED FISH RECIPES

If extra fish is provided when a meal is planned for boiled or steamed fish, or when making chowder, the unused portion of fish may be flaked and placed in the refrigerator for the following day. Many dishes that give a pleasing variety of menus may be easily prepared from these flakes.

FISH FLAKES IN CREAM (2)
(6 Servings)

2 tbsp. butter or cooking oil
1 cup cream or fish stock
3 tbsp. chopped parsley
2 tbsp. grated onion
¼ tsp. pepper
½ tsp. salt
2½ cups fish flakes

Method:
1 Put butter or oil in frying pan over a slow fire.
2 In a bowl combine other ingredients with cream.
3 Pour into fat.
4 Simmer slowly until thoroughly cooked, and seasonings are well blended.
5 Add fish flakes.
6 Serve on toast or with a baked potato.

PLAIN CREAMED FLAKES (2)
(6 Servings)

4 tbsp. melted butter
4 tbsp. flour
2 cups milk
2 lbs. flaked fish
Salt and pepper

Method:
1 Put melted butter in saucepan.
2 Stir in flour until smooth.
3 Add milk and continue stirring until the sauce thickens.
4 Add flakes.
5 Stir while heating.
6 Season as desired.

"QUICK MEAL" (2)
(6 Servings)

Method:

2 cups milk
2 tbsp. butter
½ tsp. salt
¼ tsp. pepper
2 cups coarsely crushed crackers
2 lbs. flaked salmon, bluefish, mackerel, or any other fat fish of distinctive flavor

1 Heat milk with the seasonings and butter.
2 Stir in crackers until all are wet.
3 Add fish, stirring as little as possible.

Suggestion: Two eggs well beaten may be added to the cracker mixture and mixture cooked. Then add the fish flakes. Vinegar or lemon juice may be added, if desired.

FISH FLAKE OMELETTE (2)
(6 Servings)

Method:

2 cups flaked fish
3 tbsp. vinegar or lemon juice
4 tbsp. melted butter or cooking oil
½ cup milk or fish stock
1 tsp. salt
¼ tsp. black pepper
2 tbsp. grated onion
4 egg yolks
4 egg whites

1 Mix fish and vinegar.
2 Melt butter in saucepan.
3 Add flour.
4 Add milk or stock, and seasonings.
5 Stir until smooth.
6 Add the fish flakes and beaten egg yolks.
7 Fold in stiffly beaten egg whites.
8 Pour into well oiled frying pan which has been preheated.
9 Cook slowly over low heat 2 minutes.
10 Place frying pan in 325° F. oven.
11 Cook until dry on top.
12 Remove.
13 Cut omelette on opposite sides and fold over.
14 Remove to hot platter.

FISH FLAKE SALADS (2)
(6 Servings)

Boiled fish flakes combine well with combinations of vegetables, cooked or uncooked. If careful consideration is given to flavor, the proportion of fish flakes to vegetables may be as much as half and half. The following is tasty and easily made:

Method:

2 cups boiled fish flakes
3 tbsp. spiced vinegar from sweet pickles
1 cup crisp cucumber
1 cup celery
3 red radishes, sliced thin
½ tsp. salt
Mayonnaise
Lettuce

1 Keep all ingredients cold.
2 Add vinegar to fish.
3 Let stand 10 minutes.
4 Combine the fish, diced cucumber, minced celery, sliced unpeeled radishes, and seasonings.
5 Mix with mayonnaise.
6 Fill nests of lettuce leaves with the mixture.
7 Sprinkle with a dash of paprika.

FISH IMPERIAL (2)
(6 Servings)

2 cups cooked fish flakes
3 tbsp. vinegar
3 egg yolks
½ cup milk
½ cup fish stock
1 tsp. salt
¼ tsp. black pepper
2 tbsp. grated onion
2 tbsp. parsley, chopped fine
3 egg whites
1 pimiento, sliced in strips

Method:
1 Combine fish flakes and vinegar.
2 Beat egg yolks.
3 Add milk, fish stock, seasonings and fish flakes.
4 Fold in stiffly beaten egg whites
5 Pour into greased baking dish.
6 Garnish with strips of pimiento.
7 Set in pan water.
8 Bake at 300° F. 45 minutes.

FISH PIE (2)
(6 Servings)

1 cup medium white sauce
2 cups cooked fish flakes, coarse
1 tbsp. grated onion
1 tbsp. minced green pepper
¾ cup peas
1 cup mashed potatoes
White Sauce:
2 tbsp. fat
2 tbsp. flour
¼ tsp. salt
1 cup milk

Method:
1 Blend fat and flour in saucepan.
2 Add salt and milk, stirring constantly until thick.
3 Add fish, onion, green pepper, and peas.
4 Place in a greased baking dish.
5 Cover with mashed potatoes.
6 Bake at 400° F. for 12 minutes.

HASH SUPREME (2)
(6 Servings)

2 cups cold cooked fish (large flakes)
4 tbsp. garlic vinegar
¼ cup salt pork, diced
¾ cup onion diced
1 cup cooked beets (diced)
¼ tsp. pepper
½ tsp. salt
2½ cups cooked potatoes, diced
¼ cup cold water

Method:
1 Mix vinegar and fish flakes.
2 Fry the pork to a golden brown.
3 Add the onions, and cook until yellow.
4 Add all of the ingredients.
5 Cover and let cook slowly.
6 Stir occasionally until thoroughly heated through and the flavors are blended.

FISH SOUFFLE (2)
(6 Servings)

2 cups well seasoned mashed potatoes, consistency of white sauce
2 cups cold cooked fish
½ tsp. salt
½ tsp. pepper
2 tbsp. grated onion
2 tbsp. grated carrot
4 egg yolks
4 egg whites

Method:
1 Prepare the potatoes.
2 Mix the fish flakes with the seasoning—salt, pepper, onion, and carrots.
3 Add beaten egg yolks, and potatoes.
4 Fold in egg whites beaten stiff.
5 Put in a greased baking dish.
6 Set in a pan of warm water
7 Bake slowly for 30 minutes.

SCALLOPED FISH (8)
(6 Servings)

¾ cup cracker or bread crumbs
1 cup fish flakes
Pepper and salt to taste
1 tsp. Worcestershire sauce
1 tbsp. butter

Method:
1 Use alternate layers of bread crumbs and fish.
2 Dot bread crumbs with butter.
3 Moisten with milk.
4 Bake until light brown.

FISH CROQUETTES (4)
(6 Servings)

Left-over fish (fried, baked, broiled or boiled)
Onion
Salt and pepper
1 cup mashed potatoes
1 egg beaten
Bread crumbs

Method:
1 Left-over fish may be used.
2 Pick out bones, run through grinder with a little onion.
3 Season with salt and pepper.
4 Mix 1 cup of above with 1 cup mashed potatoes.
5 Mould into balls.
6 Dip in bread crumbs, beaten egg, and crumbs.
7 Fry brown.
8 Drain on crushed paper.

FISH CROQUETTES—Pickle Sauce (5)
(6 Servings)

1½ cups cooked fish
1 cup thick white sauce
Bread crumbs
1 egg
Fat
Salt and pepper, if desired

Method:
1 Mix cooked fish with white sauce.
2 Season to taste.
3 Cool.
4 Shape into croquettes.
5 Fry in crumbs, egg and crumbs.
6 Fry in deep fat until golden brown.
7 Drain on crushed paper.

Pickle Sauce

1 tbsp. butter
1 tbsp. flour
1 cup milk
Salt and pepper
¼ cup chopped pickle

Method:
1 Melt butter
2 Stir in flour.
3 Slowly add milk.
4 Cook until done.
5 Season with salt and pepper, and add chopped pickle.

FISH FRITTERS (5)
(6 Servings)

1½ cups flour
2 tsp. baking powder
½ tsp. salt
¼ tsp. pepper
2/3 cup milk
1 egg
1½ cups flaked fish
Fat

Method:
1 Mix flour with baking powder, salt, and pepper.
2 Add milk to beaten egg.
3 Combine mixture.
4 Add flaked fish.
5 Drop by spoonfuls into hot fat.
6 Fry brown and serve with any desired sauce.
7 Drain on crushed paper.

FISH CUPS WITH EGGS (5)
(6 Servings)

1 cup cooked flaked fish
1 cup mashed potatoes
1 egg
  Bacon

Method:

1 Mix flaked fish, mashed potatoes, and egg.
2 Shape mixture into six cakes.
3 Wrap strip of bacon around each cake and fasten with a toothpick.
4 Make a depression in each cake, and drop in it a raw egg.
5 Bake in hot oven until egg is cooked.

FISH A LA KING (5)
(6 Servings)

3 tbsp. butter
3 tbsp. flour
2 cups milk
½ cup chopped mushrooms
2 cups fish flakes
½ cup diced celery
1 chopped pimiento
2 tbsp. lemon juice
  Salt, pepper, paprika
¼ tsp. nutmeg
1 egg, beaten

Method:

1 Mix butter and flour in saucepan.
2 Slowly add milk, stirring constantly.
3 When thickened, add mushrooms, celery, pimiento, lemon juice, and fish.
4 Season with salt, pepper, paprika, and nutmeg.
5 Just before serving, add well beaten egg.
6 Serve on toast.

RED FRIDAY (5)
(6 Servings)

Fish
Tomato sauce
White rice
Mushrooms

Method:

1 If fresh fish is used, cook in boiling salted water 20 minutes.
2 Heat the fish in well seasoned tomato sauce.
3 Pour mixture over cooked white rice.
4 Border with sauted or broiled mushrooms.

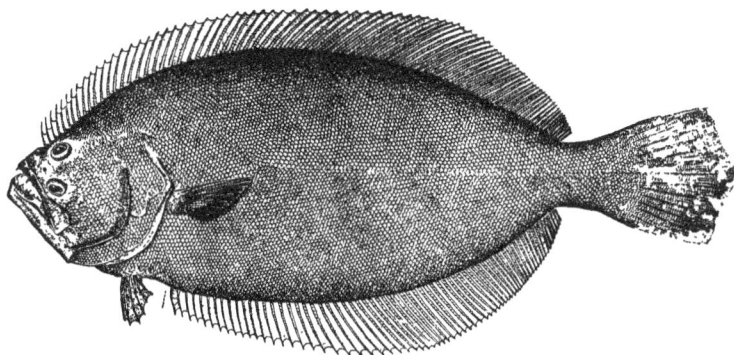

Flounder

FISH CUTLETS (5)
(6 Servings)

1 cup cooked fish
1 cup mashed potatoes
2 tbsp. minced green pepper and
   onions
   Bread crumbs

Method:
1 Mixed fish and mashed potatoes.
2 Saute minced green pepper and
   onions until soft.
8 Add to fish.
4 Season to taste.
5 Form into cutlets.
6 Dip in crumbs.
7 Fry until brown.
8 Drain on crushed paper.

FRIDAY MACARONI (5)
(6 Servings)

1 onion
2 tbsp. butter
1½ cups white sauce
2 cups cooked macaroni
1 cup cooked fish
2 pimientos (minced)
   Bread crumbs

Method:
1 Saute onion in butter.
2 Add white sauce.
8 Add macaroni, fish, and pimientos,
   minced.
4 Season to taste.
5 Cover top with crumbs.
6 Bake at 400° F. until brown.

FISH AND NOODLES—Italian (5)
(6 Servings)

1 small package noodles
2 cups cooked fish
1 can tomato soup
1 tsp. onion juice
¼ tsp. celery salt
½ tsp. salt
   Dash of pepper
   Bread crumbs

Method:
1 Cook noodles.
2 Flake cooked fish.
8 Place alternate layers fish and noodles in a baking dish, with top
   layer of noodles.
4 Add to tomato soup ready for
   serving, onion juice, celery salt,
   salt, and pepper.
5 Pour into baking dish.
6 Sprinkle top with buttered
   crumbs.
7 Bake until brown on top, or
   slowly heat on an asbestos pad on
   top of stove.

FISH LOAF WITH CREAM SAUCE (5)
(6 Servings)

1 cooked potato
1 small onion
½ green pepper
1 or 2 stalks celery
2 cups flaked fish
¼ cup dry bread crumbs
1 beaten egg
   Salt, pepper, paprika
   White sauce

Method:
1 Run through food chopper potato,
   onion, green pepper, and celery.
2 Add flaked fish, dry bread crumbs,
   beaten egg.
3 Season with salt, pepper, and paprika.
4 Mix well.
5 Shape into cylindrical loaf.
6 Roll in bread crumbs.
7 Bake in slow oven 1 hour.
8 Serve with white sauce, flavored
   with onion juice.

LENTEN PIE (5)
(6 Servings)

1 medium sized onion, minced
1 cup diced celery
1 green pepper (diced)
½ cup water
Milk
3 tbsp. butter
3 tbsp. flour
Salt and pepper
2½ cups flaked fish
Mashed potatoes

Method:

1 Boil onion, celery, and green pepper in ½ cup water
2 Drain and save water to which add sufficient milk to make 2 cups liquid
3 Melt butter
4 Stir in flour
5 Slowly add milk mixture, stirring constantly
6 Season with salt and pepper
7 Cook 3 minutes after it thickens
8 Add vegetables and fish
9 Pour in making dish
10 Cover with crust of seasoned mashed potatoes
11 Brush top with milk
12 Bake in oven until top browns

JACK HORNER'S FRIDAY PIE (5)
(6 Servings)

1 medium sized cumuber, diced
1 lb. green peas
1 bunch carrots
2 cups milk
3 tbsp. butter
3 tbsp. flour
2 cups cooked fish
Crust of pastry or biscuit dough

Method:

1 Peel and dice cucumber
2 Shell green peas
3 Slice or cube carrots
4 Cook each separately in small quantity of water
5 Drain and save water
6 Mix with milk
7 Melt butter
8 Add flour
9 Slowly add the liquid and cook
10 Mix vegetables, fish, and sauce
11 Pour in oiled baking dish
12 Cover with crust of pastry or biscuit dough
13 Brush top with milk
14 Bake at 400° F. until crust is cooked

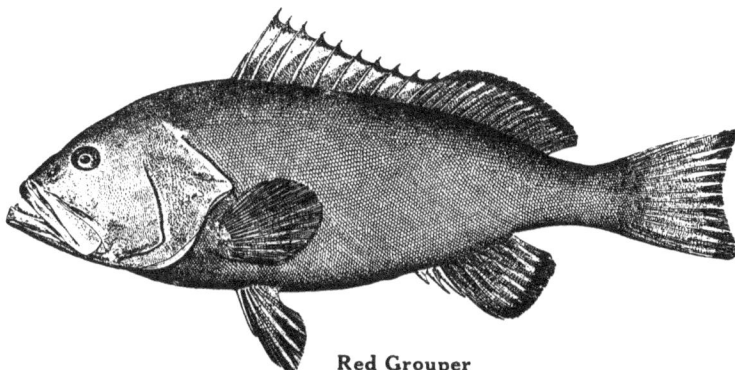

Red Grouper

EELS

Eels vary in size from the ¼-pound shoestrings to 10-pound flounders. Fresh water eels are most popular, and conger or sea eels are also used. They are sold by the pound alive, killed, smoked, and pickled. Fresh eels are skinned, sliced and generally sauted.

JELLIED EELS (5)
(6 Servings)

1 large eel
2 bay leaves
8 whole allspice, (or ½ tsp. if ground)
6 cloves
¼ tsp. pepper
½ tsp. salt
1 tbsp. gelatin
2 tbsp. cold water

Method:

1 Cut one large eel into 2-inch pieces
2 Cover with cold water and cook, bringing to boiling point
3 Skim
4 Add leaves, allspice, cloves, pepper and salt
5 Simmer until tender
6 Add gelatin soaked in cold water
7 Arrange in oiled fancy mold
8 Strain liquid through cloth
9 Cook 10 minutes
10 Cool and pour liquid over fish
11 Chill until jellied

FRIED EELS (5)
(6 Servings)

Eels
Salt
Lemon juice
Flour
Egg
Bread crumbs, (or salted milk and flour)
Tartar sauce or tomato sauce

Method:

1 Skin, bone and cut the eels into 3-inch pieces
2 Sprinkle with salt and lemon juice
3 Let stand for one hour
4 Dip in flour and beaten egg and crumbs, or in salted milk and flour
5 Saute until golden brown in color
6 Serve with tartar sauce or tomato sauce

BAKED EEL SLICES (5)

¼ cup dry bread crumbs
1 tbsp. grated cheese
Parsley
Onion (minced)
Flour
Salt
Pepper
Fat
Spinach

Method:

1 Mixed bread crumbs with grated cheese, chopped parsley, minced onion, and flour
2 Season with salt and pepper
3 Dip slices of eel in this and place in a shallow baking dish which has been oiled
4 Carefully pour melted fat or oil over each slice
5 Bake until done, about 30 minutes
6 Serve on a bed of spinach

CLAMS

In purchasing clams, examine carefully to see that they have shells tightly held together, proving that they are alive. If time allows, place them in a shallow pan about three hours before opening and sprinkle a handful of corn meal over them. They will absorb this, and work out sand which may be held in the shell. Scrub the clams carefully with a hard, stiff brush and rinse thoroughly. To open a live clam, hold it in the palm of the hand with the shell hinge outward. Insert a slender, strong, sharp knife between the shells and cut around the clam through the muscle, twisting the knife slightly to pry open the shell. Separate the clam meats from the liquor contained in the shell. Wash the meats, if necessary, to free from sand.

Another method is to place them for 10 minutes in water heated to 102° to 106° F. Hold the clam in the left hand, with the hinge outward, insert the knife about ½ inch to the side of the hinge and just deep enough to separate the shells without cutting the meat. Then twist the knife to force the shells apart, being careful not to break off a piece of the shell. The meat, intact, may then be separated from each shell.

CLAM COCKTAIL (2)
(6 Servings)

30 small clams
6 tbsp. cocktail sauce

Method:
1 Place cocktail sauce in small glass in center of each plate
2 Surround with six clams on the halfshell resting on crushed ice

CLAM BROTH (5)
(6 Servings)

2 doz. hard clams
1 cup water
6 cups liquid
Salt
Celery salt

Method:
1 Use hard clams in shell, scrub thoroughly
2 Place in kettle covered with one cup water
3 Steam until shells open
4 Strain the liquid through a cheesecloth and add enough hot water to make 6 cups of liquid
5 Season with salt and celery salt

STEAMED CLAMS (5)
(4 Servings)

24 clams
½ cup of water
Butter
Lemon juice

Method:

1 Use 24 clams
2 Wash and scrub shells
3 Place in large kettle with ½ cup of water
4 Cover and steam until shells open —about 15 minutes
5 Serve on half shell, seasoned with butter and lemon juice

FLORIDA CLAM CHOWDER (4)
(6 Servings)

2 onions, medium size
2 tbsp. butter
2 large Irish potatoes
1 qt. hot water
6 large clams
Salt and pepper

Method:

1 Peel and slice onions
2 Fry in butter
3 Add hot water to potatoes (ground)
4 Boil until soft
5 Add clams
6 Season with salt and pepper
7 Cook 15 minutes
8 Serve with crackers, like soup, as first course
9 Serves 6

SARASOTA MAY DAY LUNCHEON CLAM CHOWDER (4)
(20 Servings)

½ lb. salt pork, chopped fine
6 potatoes, diced
4 onions, sliced
1 qt. clams, cut up or ground
2 qts. milk, preferably 2 cans evaporated milk, with water added to make desired quantity
Salt and pepper

Method:

1 Put chopped pork in kettle, try out
2 Add potatoes, onion and clams
3 Boil 10 minutes
4 Thicken to the consistency of cream, and beat
5 Immediately before serving, add hot milk
6 Season to taste with butter, pepper, and salt
7 If allowed to boil after the milk is added, it is apt to curdle

Channel Bass (Red Fish)

CLAM CHOWDER—New England Style (4)
(6 Servings)

½ lb. salt pork, diced
2 onions, chopped fine
4 potatoes, peeled and diced
2 doz. large clams, cut up or ground
2½ cups hot water
1 qt. hot milk
8 crackers

Method:
1 Fry diced pork until brown
2 Remove from pan
3 Brown onions and potatoes in fat
4 Heat clams and drain
5 Add clams to above ingredients
6 Add hot water
7 Simmer until vegetables are tender
8 Add hot milk anu crumbled crackers
9 Just before serving, pour in hot clam liquor
10 Season to taste
11 Clam liquor must be added last, as it has a tendency to make milk curdle

CLAM CHOWDER—Manhattan Style (5)
(Coney Island)
(6 Servings)

¼ lb. salt pork, diced
2 large onions
1 carrot
1 cup celery
1 green pepper
2 cups tomatoes
4 cups water
  Pinch of thyme
  Salt and pepper
2 doz. large clams, ground
  Crackers or pilot biscuit

Method:
1 Fry pork until brown
2 Remove from the pan
3 Chop onions, carrot, celery, green pepper
4 Saute in pork fat until yellow
5 Add tomatoes, water, pinch of thyme, salt and pepper
6 Simmer until tender about 10 minutes
7 Add hot clams and liquor
8 Thicken with crackers or pilot biscuit

CLAM CHOWDER SUPREME (4)
(Without Milk)
(6 Servings)

2 doz. clams in shell
6 slices salt pork, cut in small pieces
6 potatoes, diced small
6 tomatoes, sliced
4 medium onions, sliced
½ tsp. black pepper
  Dash tabasco sauce
4 thyme, 2 bay leaves
2 tarragon leaves
¼ tsp. ground cloves

Method:
1 Wash the clams, scrubbing thoroughly
2 Place in kettle with hot water
3 Cook until shells open
4 As fast as they open lift out
5 Take out the clam meat
6 Drain the juice into a bowl
7 Chop the clams in small pieces
8 Boil ingredients until salt pork and vegetables are done
9 Add the clams
10 Cook 10 minutes
11 Add the liquor from the clams
12 Serve hot

PUREE OF CLAMS (9)
(6 Servings)

25 clams
1 cup cold water
1 tbsp. butter
2 tbsp. flour
¼ cup bread crumbs
1 pt. milk
Pepper to taste

Method:
1 Drain the clams with the water, saving all the liquor
2 Put the liquor in a saucepan over the fire
3 When it comes to boil, skim
4 Chop clams fine
5 Add to the liquor
6 Let boil and skim again
7 Rub the butter and flour together, until smooth
8 Add the broth and bread crumbs
9 Stir and cook until it thickens
10 Press through a sieve
11 Return to the kettle
12 When heated, add the scalded milk
13 Season and serve at once

CLAM FRITTERS (2)
(6 Servings)

1½ doz. clams
1½ cups flour
1 tsp. salt
¼ tsp. pepper
¾ cup clam liquor
½ cup milk
3 eggs, beaten
1 tbsp. melted butter
Cooking fat

Method:
1 Separate clams from liquor
2 Split the clams, remove dark stomach contents
3 Rinse in cold water
4 Mince clams as fine as possible
5 Sift flour, salt and pepper
6 Add claim liquor, milk, and eggs
7 Stir until smooth
8 Add butter and minced clams
9 Saute in heavy frying pan in thin cakes, or drop tablespoonful in hot fat (380° F.) and cook until golden brown

CLAMS STUFFED (5)
(6 Servings)

24 Clams
4 mushrooms
2 slices bacon
½ tsp. minced parsley
Bread crumbs
Salt and pepper

Method:
1 Remove clams from shells
2 Scrub shells, and boil 2 minutes
3 Chop the clams
4 Combine clams with chopped mushrooms, diced bacon, parsley, and enough bread crumbs to hold mixture in shape
5 Season with salt and pepper
6 Fill clam shells
7 Sprinkle with crumbs
8 Dot with butter
9 Bake in moderate oven until brown on top—about 12 minutes

BERKSHIRE CLAM PIE (5)
(6 Servings)

2 cups chopped clams
2 cups cooked sliced potatoes
Flour
Minced onion and parsley
Salt and pepper
1 cup clam juice
3 tbsp. tomato juice
Pastry or biscuit crust

Method:

1 Plate layer of potatoes in baking dish
2 Follow with layer of clams
3 Dredge with flour
4 Sprinkle with minced onion and parsley
5 Season with salt and pepper
6 Repeat, with layer of potatoes on top
7 Mix clam juice and tomato juice, and pour over
8 Top with crust
9 Bake in hot oven

CLAM PIGLETS (5)
(6 Servings)

30 large clams
6 slices bacon
Clam liquor

Method:

1 Wrap slices of bacon around clams
2 Fasten with a toothpick
3 Bake in moderate oven
4 Serve 5 to a portion with clam liquor poured over

CLAMS IN SAUCE (5)
(6 Servings)

24 clams chopped
4 hard-boiled eggs, sliced
1 onion, minced
1 green pepper, diced
1 tsp. parsley, chopped
½ cup celery, diced
1 pt. white sauce

Method:

1 Mix all ingredients
2 Season to taste
3 Pour into baking dish
4 Cover top with crumbs
5 Bake until top is browned

FRIED SOFT CLAMS (5)
(6 Servings)

24 dry clams
Flour
Salt and pepper
Egg
Bread crumbs
Lemon

Method:

1 Dry 24 clams
2 Roll in flour, seasoned with salt and pepper
3 Dip in egg, then in crumbs
4 Fry until light brown. Serve with lemon

Suggestion: Clams may be dipped in batter or bread crumbs.

CONCHS

In the West Indies this mollusk grows very large and is found in quantities, but those in Florida waters are relatively small. In the Key West section conch steaks and stews are everyday items on the menus of restaurants and homemakers. This favorite univalve is easily gathered from the many island shores, and the shells are used for garden ornaments, for "horns"—a blast calling the family to dinner—and also sell readily to the tourist trade and shell collectors.

CONCH CHOWDER (10)
(6 Servings)

2 conchs
1 large slice salt pork, diced
2 large onions, minced
2 cans tomato paste
2 cloves garlic
2 qts. water
½ cup rice

Method:
1 Scald conch meat
2 Run through food chopper, using coarse blade
3 Put into salt water
4 Drain
5 Fry salt pork
6 Add onions, tomato paste and garlic
7 Cook slowly 20 minutes
8 Add water, rice and drained conch meat
9 Cook half an hour

Suggestion: This may be reheated and is better the second day.

CRABS

Several species of crabs are taken from Florida coastal waters, probably the most common being the large blue crab, easily caught by line or net as the tide comes in, and always

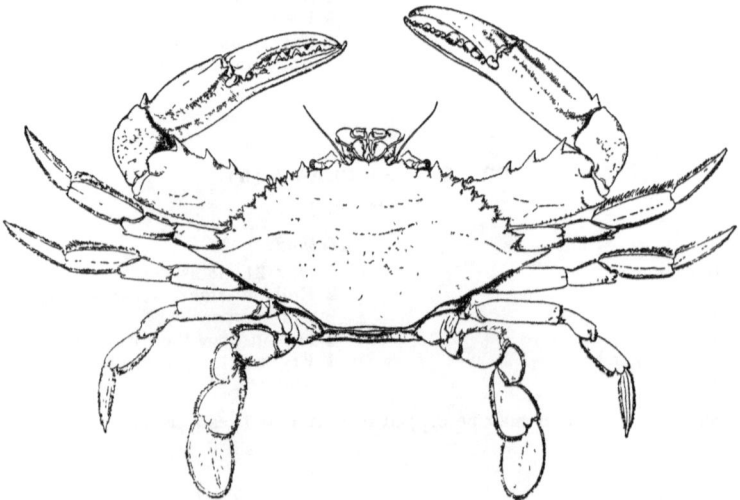

Blue Crab

available at local markets. These are the hard-shell variety and may be cooked at the shore and placed on ice, or brought home alive in buckets or barrels, or the familiar "croker" sack. Crabs should be alive when originally cooked. If the home-maker is to cook them, they must be handled with great care, unless the smaller side of the claws are unjointed. Otherwise, painful injury may result.

Scrub the crabs and steam for 25 minutes, or drop the crabs into boiling water. Boil rapidly for the first 5 minutes,

Removal of legs from cooked crabs

and simmer for 10 minutes. Remove when cool enough to handle. A delicious seasoning may be secured by boiling in a solution of the following proportions:

¼ cup vinegar	1 tbsp. red pepper
2 tbsp. salt	2 qts. water

Very sweet meat is found in the claws, legs, and body of the crab. Pull off the claws and legs, and crack the shells. Break off the segment that folds under the body from the rear. Hold the crab in the left hand, with back toward you. Slip the fingers of the right hand under the top shell and pull the body downward without breaking. This will release the top shell which is used for baking deviled crabs. Under the faucet remove the digestive tract; split the central crease. In the left hand hold half of the body and with a sharp knife cut out the hard membranous covering along the outer edge. With a nut-pick, remove the tender sweet muscles in each cavity. Be careful not to break off pieces of the shell into the crab meat. Pick out the meat carefully to avoid washing the meat after removal, because of loss of flavor as well as food value. Use only unchipped porcelain, china, or glass dishes in which to place the crab meat.

Slicing the body of the Crab to make easy the removal of the meat

SOFT-SHELLED CRABS (2)

The commercial soft-shelled crab is usually the blue crab taken immediately after molting and before the shell hardens. Use only live crabs.

To Dress :
1. Use a sharp knife to cut off the segments that fold under the rear of the body.
2. Turn the crab about and cut off the face from ½ to ¾ inch back of the eyes.
3. Lift each point at the sides and remove all of the gills.
4. Wash the crab.

To Cook:
1. Put the fat to heat in an iron kettle.
2. Salt by dipping the crab into a solution made of 2 tbsp. of salt dissolved in 1 cup of water.
3. Let stand from one to two minutes.
4. Remove, and let drip.
5. Place in a wire basket one layer deep.
6. Cook at 365° F. until a golden brown.

7. Turn while cooking.
8. Remove, drain fat on crushed paper.
9. Serve with tartar sauce.
10. The entire crab is edible.

Another Method:
1. Dip the soft-shelled crabs in beaten egg seasoned with salt and pepper.
2. Roll in flour, corn meal, or dip in light batter.
3. Fry brown in deep fat or oil.
4. Serve on toast or sauted bread with tartar sauce.

CRAB MEAT COCKTAIL (2)

Method:

Flaked crab meat
¼ cup tomato catsup
2 tbsp. lemon juice
1 tbsp. grated horseradish
1 tbsp. finely minced celery
¼ tsp. salt
3 drops tabasco sauce

1 Put the necessary amount of flaked crab meat in cocktail glasses or sherbet cups (2 to 3 tbsp.)
2 Chill thoroughly.
3 Serve sauce of remaining ingredients.

GEORGIA CRAB MEAT STEW (9)
(3 Servings)

Method:

1 tbsp. butter
1 tbsp. flour
1 pt. milk
Salt and pepper to taste
Meat from 6 crabs
2 tbsp. sherry wine

1 Melt butter.
2 Add flour
3 When bubbling add milk, salt, and pepper.
4 Let come to boil.
5 Add crab meat, and remove from fire.
6 When stew is in dish, add 2 tbsp. sherry.

CRAB MEAT SALAD (2)
(6 Servings)

Method:

1 head lettuce
2 cups crab meat
Juice of one lemon
Salt and pepper
Mayonnaise

1 Arrange lettuce in six nests about 4 inches across.
2 Mix crab meat, lemon juice, seasoning as desired, and enough mayonnaise to hold the crab meat together when pressed into a small cup.
3 Invert the contents of the cup into a lettuce nest.
4 Repeat.
5 Top with a spoonful of mayonnaise.

Suggestion: One cup of chopped celery, apple, hard-boiled egg, olives, etc., may be mixed with the crab meat, if desired.

SARASOTA CRAB FLAKE SALAD (4)
(8 Servings)

1 cup stiff mayonnaise
2 cups crab flakes
1 cup celery (diced)
1 cup cucumbers, diced
2 hard-boiled eggs, sliced
2 tbsp. chopped sweet pickle
2 tbsp. lemon juice
½ tsp. salt
Pimientos may be added if desired.

Suggestion: Pimientos may be added.

Method:
1 Mix the mayonnaise with the crab flakes, celery, cucumbers, eggs, sweet pickles, lemon juice, and salt.
2 Chill in refrigerator.
3 Serve in a large bowl lined with lettuce.
4 Top with the remaining mayonnaise.
5 Serve at once.

APALACHICOLA CRAB MEAT SALAD (11)
(6 Servings)

1 tbsp. lemon juice
2 tbsp. mayonnaise
½ cup diced celery
1 cup crab meat
Salt and paprika

Method:
1 Mix the lemon juice and mayonnaise.
2 Add the crab meat and celery, with salt and paprika to taste.
3 Serve on crisp lettuce.
4 Garnish with slice of tomato and hard-boiled eggs, with a spot of mayonnaise and a dash of paprika in center.

APALACHICOLA CRAB CHOWDER (11)
(6 Servings)

¼ lb. salt pork, diced
2 tbsp. onion, minced
3 cups potatoes, diced
1 pt. water
2 lbs. crab meat
1 pt. hot milk
1 tbsp. cornstarch
Salt and pepper

Method:
1 Cook the salt pork in the bottom of the chowder kettle until it is a golden color.
2 Add the onion and cook until it is soft and yellow.
3 Add the potatoes.
4 Cover with pint of water.
5 Simmer until the potatoes are done.
6 Add the crab meat.
7 Allow to simmer for a short period.
8 Add the hot milk thickened with cornstarch.
9 Season with salt and pepper to taste and serve.

CREOLE CRAB MEAT JAMBALAYA (12)
(6 Servings)

2 small onions
2 tbsp. parsley
½ bell pepper
1 tbsp. butter or fat
1 clove garlic
1 small can tomatoes
1 cup cooked rice
1 lb. crab meat (claws)
2 cups water
Salt and pepper to taste

Method:
1 Chop onions, parsley and bell pepper.
2 Brown in melted butter or fat.
3 Stir well.
4 Add garlic.
5 Fry for a few minutes.
6 Add tomatoes and cooked rice, crab meat and water.
7 Add salt and pepper, and heat.
8 Serve hot.

FLORIDA CRAB MEAT CANAPE (1)
(6 Servings)

½ cup flaked crab meat
2 tbsp. butter
1 tbsp. mayonnaise
2 tbsp. grated cheese
6 slices toast

Method:
1 Mix the crab meat, butter, mayonnaise and seasoning.
2 Spread on toast cut in oblong shapes.
3 Sprinkle with grated cheese.
4 Serve.

FLORIDA CRAB CUTLETS (1)
(6 Servings)

2 tbsp. butter
2 tbsp. flour
½ cup milk
1 cup crab meat
1 egg yolk
1 tsp. finely chopped parsley
Few grains cayenne pepper
Few grains nutmeg
Bread crumbs
1 egg white

Method:
1 Melt butter.
2 Add flour.
3 When well mixed add milk slowly, stirring until it boils.
4 Mix crab meat with seasoning and egg yolk.
5 Add as much white sauce as the mixture will take up, being careful not to let it get too soft.
6 Spread out on plate.
7 When cool, divide into six portions as you would for a pie.
8 Shape each in the form of a cutlet.
9 Dip in fine bread crumbs, then in egg white slightly beaten with one tbsp. water.
10 Coat with crumbs again.
11 Place three at a time in frying basket.
12 Fry in hot fat 190° F. about one minute.

BOILED CRABS A LA CREOLE (12)
(6 Servings)

1 cup salt
½ cup ground pepper
2 qts. water
1 dozen crabs

Method:
1 Add salt and pepper to water.
2 When boiling add crabs.
3 Cover top of container tight so as not to let the steam escape.
4 Let boil for 20 minutes.
5 Serve, accompanied by nut crackers or small hammers.

CRAB GUMBO A LA CREOLE (12)
(6 Servings)

1 cup shortening
1 cup flour
1 small onion, chopped
¼ clove garlic
Meat from 8 crabs
Onion tops
1 cup diced celery
6 cups water
Parsley
Salt and pepper

Method:
1 Heat the shortening.
2 Add the flour.
3 Stir until brown.
4 Add chopped onions and garlic.
5 Stir until onions are soft.
6 Add the crab meat, onion tops, celery, water, salt and pepper.
7 Let simmer slowly for one hour.
8 Just before serving, add parsley and any good hot prepared sauce to improve the flavor.

STUFFED CRABS A LA CREOLE (12)
(6 Servings)

1½ dozen crabs
1 small loaf stale white bread
1 small onion
¼ clove garlic
½ cup shortening
　Salt and pepper
　Bread crumbs

Method:
1 Boil crabs 20 minutes.
2 Pick out meat.
3 Grind the bread, onions, and garlic.
4 Mix with the crab meat.
5 Heat shortening and add mixture to it.
6 When well smothered, add seasoning to taste, celery, parsley, and onion tops.
7 Fill crab shells.
8 Sprinkle with bread crumbs.
9 Bake at 400° F. for 20 minutes.

Note: Before filling crab shells, boil in salty water, using a brush to scrub them.

TOMATOES STUFFED WITH CRAB MEAT (12)
(8 Servings)

8 medium sized tomatoes
1 large tbsp. butter
1 small onion, chopped
½ bell pepper, chopped fine
1 lb. crab meat
4 slices bread
　Pepper and salt to taste

Method:
1 Remove inside of tomatoes carefully, leaving tomato cups.
2 Cook centers in saucepan with the butter.
3 Add onion and bell pepper.
4 Season highly.
5 Add four slices bread, toasted and crumbled.
6 Stuff into tomatoes.
7 Bake for 20 minutes at 400° F.

BAKED CRAB MEAT AND CELERY (12)
(10 Servings)

1 cup fat
1 cup flour
2 tsp. salt
¼ tsp. pepper
8 cups milk
6 cups flaked crab meat
3 cups cooked celery, diced
1 pimiento, chopped fine

Method:
1 Heat the fat.
2 Add flour, salt, and pepper.
3 Mix well.
4 Add milk gradually.
5 Cook over hot water until thick.
6 Stir to keep mixture smooth.
7 Add crab meat, celery, and pimiento.
8 Heat thoroughly.
9 Put in greased baking dish.
10 Sprinkle with crumbs.
11 Bake in moderate oven until crumbs are brown.

APALACHICOLA DEVILED CRAB (11)
(6 Servings)

2 tbsp. butter
2 tbsp. flour
1 cup milk
1 cup crab meat
½ tbsp. finely minced onion
1 tbsp. Worcestershire sauce
White pepper and red pepper to taste
Bread crumbs
2 tbsp. melted butter
½ cup cheese, grated

Method:
1 Melt butter.
2 Add flour.
3 Scald milk.
4 Add slowly to mixture.
5 Add crab meat and seasoning, stirring constantly.
6 Beat until smooth.
7 Fill empty, well cleaned shells.
8 Sprinkle with bread crumbs, melted butter and cheese.
9 Bake in shallow pan about 10 minutes in over 500° F.

MIAMI DEVILED CRABS (1)
(6 Servings)

5 tbsp. butter
8 tbsp. flour
¾ cup hot milk
1 tsp. chopped parsley
Salt and pepper
1 tsp. Lea and Perrin's Sauce
2 tsp. Sherry wine (may be omitted)
1 beaten egg
2 hard-boiled eggs, chopped
1 cup flaked crab meat
½ cup buttered bread crumbs

Method:
1 Melt butter.
2 Stir in flour.
3 Gradually add milk, seasoning and well beaten egg.
4 Stir in chopped hard-boiled egg, crab meat, and buttered bread crumbs.
5 Pile lightly in washed shells.
6 Sprinkle generously with the buttered crumbs.
7 Bake until crumbs are brown.

CRAB MEAT AU GRATIN (1)
(6 Servings)

3 tbsp. butter
3 tbsp. flour
1 cup hot milk or cream
¼ tsp. onion juice
½ tsp. Lea and Perrin's sauce
Salt and pepper to taste
1½ cups crab meat
½ cup buttered bread crumbs

Method:
1 Melt the butter.
2 Stir in the flour.
3 Add hot milk, seasoning and crab meat.
4 Fill buttered ramekins.
5 Sprinkle with bread crumbs, and grated cheese.
6 Dot with butter.
7 Bake until crumbs are brown.

CRAB MEAT IN RAMEKINS (1)
(6 Servings)

4 tbsp. butter
4 tbsp. flour
2 cups hot cream
¼ tsp. paprika
Few grains salt, cayenne, and nutmeg
1 tsp. grated onion
1 tsp. finely chopped parsley
2 cups crab meat
Buttered bread crumbs

Method:
1 Melt butter in a saucepan.
2 Add flour.
3 Stir until well blended.
4 Add hot cream gradually.
5 Stir constantly until sauce is smooth.
6 Season with salt, cayenne, nutmeg, paprika, grated onion, finely chopped parsley.
7 Heat crab meat in sauce.
8 Turn mixture into ramekins.
9 Cover with buttered bread crumbs.
10 Bake in hot oven until crumbs are brown.

SARASOTA CRAB CROQUETTES (4)
(8 Servings)

4 tbsp. butter
6 tbsp. flour
2 cups milk
1 egg yolk
2 cups crab meat   (½ lb.)
½ tsp. salt
2 tbsp. chopped parsley
2 tbsp. chopped celery
2 tbsp. chopped pimiento

Method:
1 Melt the butter.
2 Add the flour
3 Add the milk.
4 Cook until sauce is thick.
5 Add remainder of ingredients.
6 Mix well.
7 Cool.
8 Take tbsp. of mixture, roll in crumbs, then in egg, and again in crumbs.
9 Shape into balls 1½ inches in diameter.
10 Flatten to resemble a small pumpkin.
11 Fry in deep fat until well browned.
12 Insert tiny stem of parsley.

CRAB MEAT AND TOMATO A LA SARASOTA (4)
(6 to 8 Servings)

2 cups canned tomatoes
2 whole cloves
1 small onion, minced
1 tsp. celery seed
1 tsp. salt
1/8 tsp. pepper
2 tbsp. sugar
1 tbsp. lemon juice
1 tbsp. gelatin
2 tbsp. cold water
1 cup cream
1 green pepper
1 cup crab meat

Method:
1 Combine the tomatoes, cloves, onion, celery seed, salt, pepper and sugar.
2 Let simmer 15 minutes.
3 Strain
4 Add lemon juice and gelatin which has been softened in water until dissolved.
5 Cool until mixture begins to set.
6 Beat with an egg beater until frothy.
7 Fold in the cream beaten stiff, the green pepper seeded and chopped fine, and the crab meat.
8 Turn into the freezing tray and chill.
9 Do not allow to freeze.
10 Cut in 1½ inch squares and serve on crisp lettuce leaf.
11 Garnish with mayonnaise or boiled dressing.
12 This may also be packed into closed container and frozen in ice and salt—4 parts ice to 1 part salt.

CRAB ENCHILADA
(Serving for 4)

½ pint olive oil
1 large onion
2 bell peppers
1 No. 2 can tomatoes
2 No. 1 cans tomato puree
2 small cans tomato sauce
1 dozen crabs
Salt and hot red pepper to taste.

Method:
Chop onion and bell peppers. Fry in oil until brown. Add tomatoes, puree and sauce. Cook on slow fire for one hour. Add crabs and cook for another hour or hour and a half.

SARASOTA CRAB MEAT CHOW MEIN (4)
(4 Servings)

4 tbsp. butter
1 lb. crab meat
1 cup chicken stock
1 tbsp. cornstarch
2 tbsp. fat
1 onion
1 bunch celery
1 tsp. salt
¼ tsp. pepper
Few grains cayenne pepper
1/3 box noodles
1 bottle Soya sauce

Method:

1 Melt butter.
2 Add crab meat.
3 Cook for 5 minutes.
4 Add cup of chicken stock mixed with cornstarch.
5 Simmer 3 minutes.
6 In another frying pan put 2 tbsp. fat, onion cut lengthwise in fine pieces, and celery cut in narrow strips 2 inches long.
7 Cook 3 minutes.
8 Drain boiled noodles.
9 Brown in butter.
10 Combine all mixtures and seasonings.
11 Serve with Soya sauce.

CRAB CAKES (4)
(6 Servings)

1 lb. crab meat
4 tbsp. melted butter
½ tsp. salt
¼ tsp. black pepper
Pinch of cayenne pepper
2 eggs well beaten
Fine bread crumbs
Cooking fat or oil

Method:

1 Mix crab meat, butter, seasoning, and enough of the egg to mold into small flat cakes.
2 Beat 1 tbsp. water into the remaining egg and dip the cakes into this mixture.
3 Roll in crumbs.
4 Saute until rich brown in a heavy frying pan or fry in deep fat at 380° F.
5 Use wire basket for deep fat.

CRAB MEAT DIXIE (5)
(6 Servings)

3 tbsp. minced onion
4 tbsp. butter
3 tbsp. flour
1 cup crab meat
2 cups milk

Method:

1 Saute minced onion in butter until beginning to brown.
2 Add flour.
3 Cook to golden brown.
4 Add crab meat and milk, stirring constantly.
5 Cook about 3 minutes.
6 Season to taste.
7 Pour over hot split biscuits.

DEVILED CRAB IN PEPPER CASES (5)
(6 Servings)

6 green peppers
3 tbsp. butter
2 tbsp. flour
1 tsp. dry mustard
1 cup milk
1 cup crab meat
1 cup soft bread crumbs
1 tsp. lemon juice
Season to taste

Method:
1 Cut peppers in half.
2 Remove seeds.
3 Steam for 5 minutes.
4 Cook butter and flour.
5 When bubbling add mustard and milk.
6 Bring to boil.
7 Add crab meat, bread crumbs, lemon juice, and seasoning.
8 Fill peppers with mixture.
9 Cover with buttered crumbs.
10 Place in shallow baking dish with ¼ inch water.
11 Bake 20 minutes at 400° F.

MIAMI CRAB AND AVOCADO SALAD (13)
(6 Servings)

6 cooked artichoke hearts
6 tbsp. French dressing
3 large avocados
2 cups crab meat
½ tsp. salt
Special salad dressing (below)
1 pimiento
2 tomatoes

Method:
1 Marinate artichoke hearts for an hour in the French dressing.
2 Peel avocados and cut in half with a sharp knife, making a sawtooth edge.
3 Remove pits.
4 Mix crab meat with salt and special dressing.
5 Place one artichoke heart in each half of avocado.
6 Surround with crab meat.
7 Arrange each avocado in a bed of crisp lettuce.
8 Top with strips of pimiento.
9 Surround with small wedges of tomato.

Special Dressing:
1 cup mayonnaise
1 tbsp. finely minced green pepper
2 tsp. grated onion
3 tbsp. lemon juce
1 tsp. Worcestershire sauce

Method:
1 Mix all ingredients together.

Snook (Robalo)

STONE CRAB

Stone crabs are popular with Floridians and Florida visitors, and are featured on restaurant and hotel menus. Peculiarly, the habitat of the stone crab in the Gulf of Mexico does not extend north of the Pinellas Keys terminating at Anclote light. Consequently, it provides a dish to be found in somewhat restricted area during the late fall and winter.

A State law prohibits the shipment of these stone crabs from Florida, and an act of the 1935 Legislature prohibits their capture in waters at the southern end of the peninsula around Key West.

The huge claws, filled with rich meat, are the only part eaten.

To Cook:
1. Boil in salt water 20 minutes.

To Serve:
1. Crack with a hammer.
2. Extract the meat and dip in melted butter.
3. The meat may also be extracted before serving and prepared in salads and other dishes.

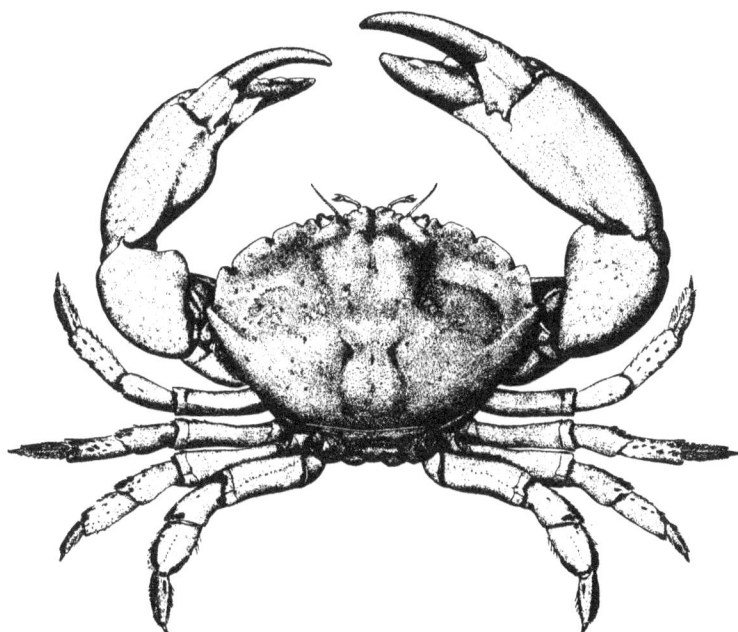

Stone Crab

CRAWFISH (Florida Lobster)

This Southern species, a "spiny" lobster, found off the southern Florida coasts and among the keys, is distinguished from the northern variety by the absence of claws and the presence of two long antenna protruding from the head.

If possible, lobsters should be alive when the cooking process is started.

1.   Place the lobster on its back on a cutting board and kill by cutting down between the body shell and tail segment.

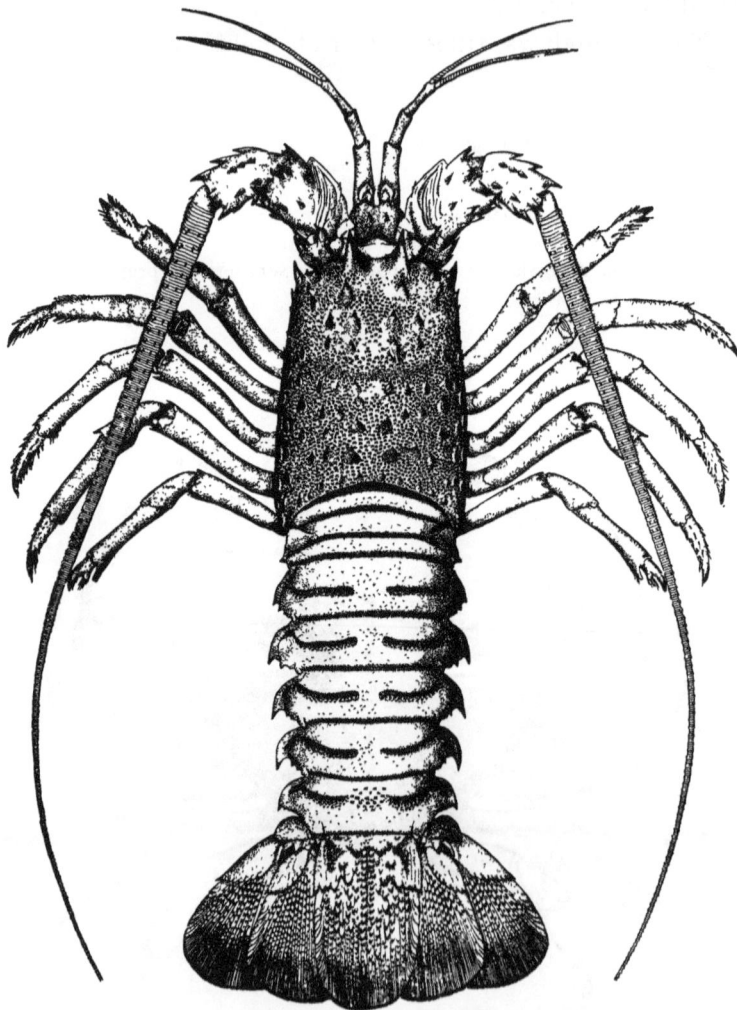

Florida Crawfish

2. Split from the head to the tail.

3. Remove fat, coral (if present), stomach, and the vein that passes through the center of the tail segment.

Or: Live lobsters may be cooked immediately by plunging them into boiling water, to which one tablespoon of salt has been added for each quart of water. Boil rapidly from three to four minutes, then simmer for about 15 minutes. The shells are then cracked open, and the meat removed. Pre-cooked lobsters or crawfish are to be found usually in first-class fish markets and may be easily prepared by any of the following recipes:

CRAWFISH STUFFED (4)
(2 Servings)

1 pre-cooked crawfish (2 lbs.)
1 tbsp. butter
2 tbsp. sherry
½ cup cream
1 cup bread crumbs (or cracker crumbs)

Method:
1 Split. as above directed, place on rack and stuff.
Dressing:
1 In one tbsp. butter cook the liver, mashing it while it cooks for four minutes.
2 Remove from heat.
3 Add 2 tbsp. sherry and ½ cup cream.
4 Add bread crumbs (or cracker crumbs)
5 Pack this stuffing into the head of the crawfish, and fill the whole shell.
6 Cook under broiler or in a hot oven for 20 minutes.

CRAWFISH WITH MUSHROOMS (4)
(8 Servings)

1 cup mushrooms
6 tbsp. butter
3 tbsp. flour
1 tsp. salt
Dash of paprika
1½ cups milk
½ cup stock
1 cup cream
2 cups crawfish meat, diced
2 egg yolks, beaten
½ cup bread crumbs (toasted)

Method:
1 Saute the mushrooms in the melted butter.
2 Add flour, salt and paprika.
3 Cook 5 minutes.
4 Add milk and stock gradually.
5 Cook 3 minutes.
6 Add the cream, crawfish and egg yolks.
7 Pour into greased casserole.
8 Cover top with crumbs and 1½ tbsp. butter.
9 Bake for 10 minutes in a very hot oven (500° F.).

CRAWFISH LOAF (4)
(6 Servings)

2 cups crawfish meat
Salt and pepper to taste
1 cup bread crumbs
1 tbsp. minced onion
½ green pepper, minced
2 eggs
½ cup milk

Method:
1 Mix crawfish, seasoning, crumbs, onion, green pepper and beaten eggs.
2 Add milk.
3 Pour in greased baking dish.
4 Bake until firm, about 30 minutes, in pan of hot water in slow oven, (325° F.)

CRAWFISH OMELETTE (4)
(Individual Serving)

1 tsp. butter
3 small onions, chopped
1 tbsp. minced celery
2 tbsp. chicken stock
½ tsp. sugar
1 tsp. Soya sauce
1/8 tsp. salt
1/8 tsp. paprika
1/3 cup diced crawfish
1 egg yolk, beaten
1 tbsp. cream
1 egg white, beaten

Method:
1 Cook butter, onions, minced celery for 3 minutes.
2 Stir frequently.
3 Add chicken stock, sugar, Soya sauce, salt, pepper and diced crawfish.
4 Add beaten yolk to the cream, and fold in the white.
5 Turn into heated omelette pan
6 When it begins to set around the edges, spread with crawfish mixture.
7 Fold over when well risen.
8 Cook for two minutes longer.
9 Turn out on a hot platter.

Suggestion: If this omelette is to be cooked quickly, heat the crawfish mixture before spreading.

CRAWFISH ENCHILADA (4)
(1 Crawfish 2 Servings)

1 crawfish
1 green pepper
1 pimiento
Olive oil
Boiled rice

Method:
1 Boil crawfish 20 minutes.
2 Pick out meat.
3 Cut in strips green pepper and pimiento.
4 Fry until tender in small amount of olive oil.
5 Add crawfish meat.
6 Serve with boiled rice.

Note: This is a favorite Key West recipe, and is considered a whole meal in itself.

CRAWFISH COCKTAIL (1)
(6 Servings)

2 cups crawfish meat
1 cup celery, cut fine
Cocktail sauce

Method:
1 Mix crawfish meat and celery.
2 Chill.
3 Serve with cocktail sauce.

CRAWFISH A LA NEWBURG (1)
(6 Servings)

2 cups crawfish meat
1 cup white sauce
1 tsp. Worcestershire sauce
1 tbsp. sherry
1 tbsp. lemon juice
1 tbsp. butter
1 cup grated cheese
  Salt and pepper to taste

Method:
1 Mix all ingredients.
2 Put in lobster shells.
  or baking dish.
3 Brown in oven.
4 Serve hot.

CRAWFISH CHOWDER (10)
(6 Servings)

2 medium crawfish
1 qt. water
3 slices bacon
1 onion, chopped fine
1 clove garlic
1 can tomatoes
2 cups raw potatoes, diced
1 bunch carrots, diced
  Salt and pepper

Method:
1 Boil crawfish 10 minutes.
2 Fry bacon.
3 Saute the onion and garlic in the
  bacon fat until brown.
4 Add tomatoes and crawfish meat.
5 Simmer 10 minutes.
6 Add 1 qt. water.
7 Add potatoes, carrots and seasonings.
8 Cook until meat and vegetables
  are tender.
9 Serve hot with crisp crackers.

BROILED CRAWFISH (1)
(2 Servings)

1 crawfish
  Salt and pepper
  Butter
  Butter sauce

Method:
1 Split boiled crawfish in half.
2 Put in baking pan.
3 Sprinkle with salt and pepper.
4 Dot with butter.
5 Bake 10 minutes.
6 Serve with butter sauce.

CRAWFISH EN CASSEROLE (1)
(6 Servings)

1½ tbsp. butter
1 tbsp. flour
1 cup milk
1 tsp. salt
½ tsp. pepper
  Dash of paprika
1½ tbsp. lemon juice
1 tbsp. chopped parsley
2 cups peas (canned may be used)
1 cup cooked crawfish
4 tbsp. bread crumbs

Method:
1 Melt butter in a saucepan.
2 Add flour.
3 When smooth add milk.
4 Stirring constantly add salt, pepper, paprika, lemon juice, parsley
  and peas.
5 Place half of sauce mixture in a
  buttered casserole.
6 Cover with crawfish.
7 Repeat.
8 Cover with crumbs.
9 Bake at 350° F. until brown.

CRAWFISH—Italian Style (5)
(6 Servings)

3 strips bacon
2 onions, minced
8 tbsp. oil
1 cup tomato sauce
1 cup cooked rice
2 small crawfish
Salt and pepper to taste

Method:
1 Saute bacon and onions in oil.
2 Add tomato sauce, rice, crawfish meat.
8 Season with salt and pepper.
4 Put into casserole or individual baking dishes.
5 Cover top with bread crumbs.
6 Bake until brown.

CRAWFISH SALAD (2)
(6 Servings)

2 cups cooked crawfish, diced
2 cups finely minced celery
Mayonnaise to mix
1 tbsp. lemon juice
Salt and paprika to taste
Lettuce

Method:
1 Chop the crawfish.
2 Mix with celery, mayonnaise, lemon juice, and seasoning.
8 Arrange lettuce in 6 nests.
4 Use a small cup as a mold, and fill with mixture; press firm.
5 Invert the molded contents into each lettuce nest.
6 Add 1 tsp. mayonnaise and paprika or crossed strips of pimiento.

Suggestion: The celery may be omitted and replaced by capers or olives.

CRAWFISH STEW (2)
(6 Servings)

1 pt. milk
1 lb. crawfish meat, boiled and coarsely diced
1½ tbsp. butter
1½ tsp. salt

Method:
1 Heat the milk to the scalding point.
2 Add meat.
8 Heat thoroughly.
4 Add butter and salt.
5 Stir well.
6 Serve hot (do not boil).

OYSTERS
SAUCE FOR RAW OYSTERS (11)
(Individual Serving)

1 tbsp. Tarragon vinegar
1 tbsp. olive oil
½ tsp. Tabasco sauce
½ tsp. salt
½ onion, grated fine

Method:
1 Mix all together.
2 Chill before serving.

OYSTER COCKTAIL (11)
(Individual Serving)

Dressing:
½ tsp. lemon juice
1 tsp. tomato catsup
Dash of Tabasco sauce
¼ tsp. salt
¼ tsp. sugar
6 oysters

Method:
1 Mix all ingredients for dressing.
2 Chill oysters and dressing.
8 Place 6 oysters in cocktail or sherbet glass.
4 Pour dressing over oysters.

OYSTER COCKTAIL IN GRAPEFRUIT (1)
(Individual Serving)

5 small oysters
½ grapefruit
Lemon juice
Salt
Tabasco sauce
1 tbsp. mayonnaise dressing
Paprika
Parsley
Saltines

Method:

1 Allow five small oysters to each person.
2 Cut medium grapefruit in halves.
3 Remove the tough center.
4 Add oysters to grapefruit halves.
5 Season each portion with lemon juice, salt, a drop or two of Tabasco sauce, and 1 tbsp. mayonnaise dressing.
6 Sprinkle with paprika.
7 Place on a bed of crushed ice.
8 Garnish with sprigs of parsley.
9 Serve with crisp saltines.

Suggestion: (Horseradish may be used in place of mayonnaise).

OYSTER SOUP (1)
(6 Servings)

1 pt. oysters
1 qt. sweet milk
2 tbsp. butter
1 tsp. salt
½ tsp. pepper

Method:

1 Heat the oysters in their liquid until they curl.
2 In a double boiler, heat the quart of milk with seasonings.
3 When ready to serve, combine the oysters and hot milk.

FRENCH OYSTER SOUP (New Orleans Style) (6)
(8 Servings)

1 qt. oysters
1 tsp. onion, minced
½ cup butter
1/3 cup flour
1 qt. milk
2 egg yolks
¾ tsp. celery salt
½ tsp. pepper

Method:

1 Clean the oysters.
2 Chop coarse, add onion.
3 Let simmer in their own juice 10 minutes.
4 Strain through cheese cloth.
5 Melt butter.
6 Add flour.
7 Stir constantly, add milk.
8 Boil 2 minutes.
9 Add oyster liquor and seasonings.
10 Pour over beaten egg yolk.
11 Serve hot.

OYSTER BOUILLON (Sarasota Style) (4)
(6 Servings)

1 pt. oysters
1 pt. cold water
1/3 tsp. celery salt
Dash of Cayenne
1 blade mace
¼ tsp. salt

Method:

1 Cook chopped oysters in their own liquor for 5 minutes.
2 Add water and seasoning.
3 When the mixture comes to a boil, strain.
4 Serve in cups with a little whipped cream.

PANNED OYSTERS (4)
(6 Servings)

1 qt. medium size oysters
1 tsp. lemon juice
Salt and pepper
Paprika
6 slices toast

Method:

1 Heat oysters until plump in their own liquid.
2 Add a tsp. lemon juice, salt, pepper, and paprika to taste.
3 Serve on toast.

STEAMED OYSTERS (4)
(6 Servings)

1 qt. fresh oysters
½ cup butter
1 tsp. grated horseradish
1 tsp. Worcestershire sauce
½ tsp. salt
1 tsp.pepper

Method:

1 Drain oysters.
2 Cook in double boiler for 10 minutes.
3 Melt butter in a saucepan.
4 Add horseradish mixed with a little water, Worcestershire sauce, salt and pepper.
5 Place oysters in a deep dish.
6 Pour the sauce over oysters.
7 Serve hot.

CREAMED OYSTERS ON TOAST (4)
(6 Servings)

1 pt. oysters
1 tbsp. butter
1 tbsp. flour
2 cups milk
½ tsp. salt
Toast

Method:

1 Scald oysters in their own liquor.
2 Do not boil.
3 Melt butter.
4 Add flour.
5 Stirring constantly, add milk, oyster liquor and salt.
6 Cook until thick and smooth.
7 Place oysters in cream sauce.
8 Serve on slices of buttered toast.

OYSTERS A LA DUXELLES
(6 Servings)

1 qt. oysters
2 tbsp. butter
4 tbsp. chopped mushrooms
2 tbsp. flour
Salt and pepper
1 egg yolk
1 tsp. lemon juice
Crackers

Method:

1 Heat oysters to the boiling point.
2 Skim and drain.
3 Reserve the liquor.
4 Melt butter in saucepan.
5 Add chopped mushrooms.
6 Cook 2 minutes.
7 Add flour, pour the hot liquor in slowly.
8 Season to taste and pour over the beaten yolk of egg and the lemon juice.
9 Cook until it thickens.
10 Add hot oysters.
11 Serve on toasted crackers.

OYSTERS AND CELERY SOUP (4)
(6 Servings)

1 cup diced celery
1 tbsp. chopped onion
2 tbsp. chopped pimientos
2 cups water
Dash Cayenne
Dash Tabasco Sauce
1 tbsp. butter
1 tbsp. flour
1 pint milk
1 pt. oysters
2 egg yolks
1 tsp. lemon juice

Method:
1 Cook celery and onion in water until tender.
2 Add pimientos, cayenne and Tabasco sauce.
3 Melt butter.
4 Add flour.
5 When smooth add milk.
6 Stir constantly until it boils.
7 Add oysters and celery mixture.
8 Heat until oysters curl.
9 Pour over beaten egg yolks.
10 Add lemon juice.
11 Serve at once on croustades made as follows:

Croustades:
1. Cut 3 in. slices from loaf of bread.
2. Scoop out center, leaving bread ¼ in. thick at bottom.
3. Brush inside and out with melted butter.
4. Bake to golden brown in 450° F. oven.

OYSTER AND MUSHROOM PIE (4)
(6 Servings)

¼ cup butter
2 cups dry bread crumbs
1 pt. oysters
½ tsp. salt
¼ tsp. pepper
¾ lb. fresh or canned mushrooms
2 tbsp. cream
4 tbsp. oyster liquor

Method:
1 Butter casserole dish—glass, if possible.
2 Spread 1 cup bread crumbs over bottom.
3 Put in oysters.
4 Dot with butter, add seasoning.
5 Add a few crumbs, mushrooms, sliced.
6 Dot with butter.
7 Pour cream and oyster liquor over mixture.
8 Cover with layer of bread crumbs.
9 Bake in moderate oven until oysters curl—30 to 40 minutes.

FRIED OYSTERS—Sarasota Style (4)
(6 Servings)

3 doz. oysters, with liquor
Cracker crumbs
Fat

Method:
1 Roll oysters in cracker crumbs.
2 Place in refrigerator several hours.
3 Dip oysters in their own liquor.
4 Roll again in cracker crumbs.
5 Fry immediately in deep fat.
6 If wire basket is not available, use perforated skimmer to remove oyster from fat.

FRIED OYSTERS—Regular (2)
(6 Servings)

3 doz. large oysters
Salt and pepper
2 eggs
1 cup fine cracker crumbs or yellow
corn meal
Cooking oil

Method:
1 Drain oysters.
2 Press between absorbent cloths.
3 Season oysters with salt and pepper.
4 Dip in beaten egg, then dry crumbs, or meal.
5 Place single layer of oysters in oiled frying basket.
6 Fry to golden brown.

OYSTERS AU GRATIN (4)
(6 Servings)

1 tbsp. butter
1 tbsp. flour
1 cup milk
Salt and pepper
3 doz. oysters
Bread crumbs

Method:
1 Heat 1 tbsp. butter in saucepan.
2 Add flour.
3 Mix and add slowly milk, season with salt and pepper.
4 Cook until sauce thickens.
5 Butter individual dishes or one large baking dish.
6 Put in layer of sauce and one of oysters, season with salt and pepper.
7 Repeat.
8 Cover with bread crumbs.
9 Dot with butter.
10 Bake in a quick oven.

Variations: A tbsp. of chopped parsley and 2 tbsp. grated cheese improves flavor of the sauce. Worcestershire sauce or anchovy sauce may be used.

OYSTER PIE (4)
(6 Servings)

3 doz. oysters
Salt, pepper, and butter
1 cup bread crumbs in milk
2 well beaten eggs
Pie crust

Method:
1 Fill a baking dish with oysters.
2 Sprinkle with salt and pepper, and bits of butter.
3 Soak bread crumbs in milk, with well beaten eggs.
4 Add to oysters.
5 Cover the dish with layer of pie crust, leaving an opening in center for steam to escape.
6 Bake at 450° F. until brown.

OYSTERS AND SPAGHETTI (4)
(6 Servings)

½ package of spaghetti
Boiling water
3 doz. oysters
Butter, salt, and pepper
1 cup milk
Cracker crumbs

Method:
1 Break a half package of spaghetti into boiling water.
2 Cook 30 minutes.
3 Drain and run cold water over it.
4 Place in buttered baking dish layers of spaghetti and oysters.
5 Season with butter, salt, and pepper.
6 Pour milk over mixture.
7 Cover with cracker crumbs.
8 Bake in hot oven 20 to 30 minutes.

PIGS IN BLANKETS (4)
(Individual Serving)

Method:

Oysters
Salt and pepper
Slice of bacon
Fat
Buttered toast

1 Season fine large oysters with salt and pepper.
2 Wrap each in a slice of bacon.
3 Fasten with a toothpick.
4 Fry in hot fat.
5 Do not burn.
6 Serve on oblong slices of buttered toast.

SCALLOPED OYSTERS (2)
(6 Servings)

Method:

1 qt. oysters, with liquor
Coarse cracker crumbs
Salt and pepper
¼ cup butter
Milk

1 Separate oysters from liquor.
2 Oil baking dish.
3 Place in it a layer of crumbs about ¼ inch thick, then layer of oysters with bits of butter.
4 Repeat.
5 Do not have more than two layers.
6 Add strained oyster liquor and milk until moisture shows.
7 Bake at 450° F. until top is well browned—about 20 min.

OYSTERS IN PARCHMENT (2)
(2 Servings)

Method:

1 doz. oysters
4 tbsp. oyster liquor
2 tsp. grated onion
1 tbsp. grated celery
2 tsp. butter
½ tsp. salt
¼ tsp. pepper
1 tsp. lemon juice
Toast

1 Oil or wet the parchment paper.
2 Put in the oysters, liquor and seasonings.
3 Bring all edges of the paper together and tie.
4 Immerse in boiling water.
5 Cook 5 to 8 minutes.
6 The oysters may be served on toast.
7 The liquid poured over them, or thickened and served as sauce.
8 This serves two persons.
9 For serving six persons, three parchment units should be prepared.
10 They may be cooked in one kettle, but the size of the unit recipe should not be enlarged.

BARBECUED OYSTERS (2)
(6 Servings)

3 doz. large oysters in shell
Bread crumbs
Paprika
¼ lb. bacon, sliced

Method:

1 Wash oyster shells thoroughly.
2 Open oysters, discard the flat shell.
3 Separate oysters from the curved shell, but allow each to remain loosely in the shell.
4 Cover oysters with bread crumbs, season with paprika.
5 Cover each oyster with bacon.
6 Place in one layer under a broiler flame until the bacon is cooked through.
7 Serves oysters hot in shells.

OYSTER CHOWDER (2)
(6 Servings)

3 tbsp. onion
3 tbsp. butter
1 cup water
¼ cup diced celery
1 qt. diced potatoes
2½ tsp. salt
¼ tsp. pepper
1 cup canned milk
3 cups water
1½ pts. small oysters

Method:

1 Saute onion in butter.
2 Add 1 cup water, celery, and potatoes.
3 Cover and cook until nearly done.
4 Season with salt and pepper.
5 When the vegetables are tender, add the milk.
6 Let come to a boil.
7 Remove from fire.
8 Add water to oysters and heat.
9 Remove any scum.
10 When edges curl, combine with milk and vegetables.
11 Let stand few minutes for flavors to blend.
12 Serve hot.

STEWED OYSTERS (11)
(3 Servings)

1 pt. water, salt, pepper
1 tbsp. rolled-cracker crumbs
3 doz. oysters
½ pt. milk

Method:

1 Put into saucepan water, salt, pepper, and rolled cracker crumbs.
2 Let come to a boil.
3 Pour in oysters.
4 Cook 30 seconds.
5 Remove from fire.
6 Pour into dish containing ½ pt. hot milk.
7 Serve immediately.
8 Do not allow the oysters to cook in the milk.

ANGELS ON HORSEBACK (11)
(8 Servings)

2 doz. oysters
Breakfast bacon
Skewers
Batter
Triangular toast pieces without
crust
Batter:
1 cup sifted flour
1 egg well beaten
½ tsp. salt
½ cup milk
1 tsp. baking powder

Method:
1 Wrap each oyster in very thin slice of bacon.
2 Place 3 oysters on steel skewer.
3 Allow 1 inch space between oysters.
4 Dip in batter.
5 Fry in deep fat.
6 Do not remove skewer.
7 Serve hot on toast.

OYSTER POT PIE (11)
(6 Servings)

1 pt. oysters
1 cup water
1 tbsp. butter
Salt and Cayenne
1 tbsp. flour
Biscuit dough

Method:
1 Put oysters into saucepan with water.
2 Heat slowly, adding butter, salt and Cayenne.
3 Thicken with flour.
4 Cook 6 minutes stirring gently.
5 Have ready light biscuit dough, cut in squares.
6 Drop them in and boil until they are cooked through.
7 If preferred, this dish may be baked in oven with top crust.

OYSTER PATES (Patties) (11)
(6 Servings)

1 qt. oysters
½ pt. rich drawn butter sauce
Salt and Cayenne pepper
Pastry shells

Method:
1 Chop oysters fine.
2 Make sauce and season with salt and Cayenne pepper.
3 Stir in the oysters, cook 5 minutes.
4 Pour into pastry shells, bake 2 minutes.
5 Serve immediately.

OYSTER FRITTERS (11)
(6 Servings)

1 qt. oysters
2 eggs
1 cup milk
2 cups flour
½ tsp. salt
1 tsp. baking powder
Cooking fat

Method:
1 Chop oysters fine.
2 Add beaten eggs.
3 Add milk.
4 Sift all dry ingredients together.
5 Add to oyster mixture.
6 Fry in deep fat like doughnuts.
7 Drain on crushed paper.

OYSTER FRITTERS (Whole) (11)
(6 Servings)

1 pt. oysters
1 cupful milk
2 eggs, well beaten
½ tsp. salt
¼ tsp. pepper
Flour to make stiff batter
Fat

Method:

1 Drain oysters.
2 Boil liquor.
3 Skim.
4 To liquor add enough water to make one cupful.
5 Add milk, eggs, salt, pepper, and enough flour to make a stiff batter.
6 Add whole oysters to batter.
7 Have ready kettle of hot fat.
8 Take up batter by spoonfuls, taking one oyster each time, and drop carefully into fat.
9 Fry to golden brown.
10 Drain upon paper laid in wire basket.

CLUBHOUSE OYSTERS (15)
(Individual Serving)

Slices of bread, toasted
Butter
4 large oysters
Salt, pepper and butter
Egg whites, beaten stiff
1 large tsp. slightly salted whipped cream

Method:

1 Toast as many slices of bread as are desired for serving.
2 Butter toast.
3 Place on each piece of toast 4 large oysters.
4 Season with salt, pepper and butter.
5 Return to oven.
6 When the oysters are sizzling hot and the edges curled, cover with a mound of egg whites beaten stiff.
7 Make a depression in each egg white mound.
8 Return to the oven and brown slightly.
9 Place a large tsp. of slightly salted whipped cream in each mound.
10 Serve at once.

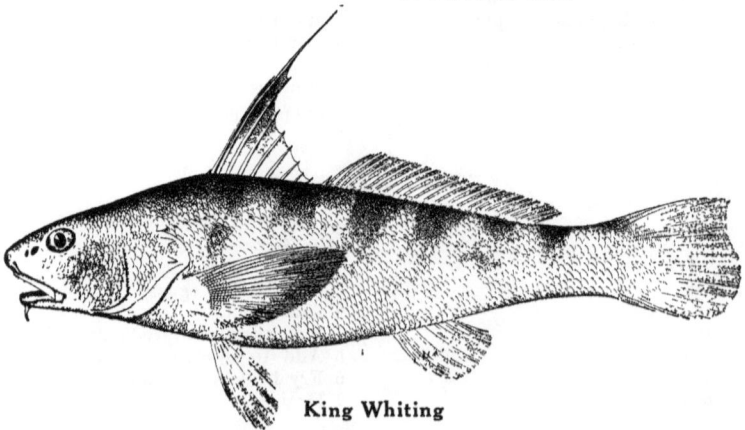

King Whiting

FILE GUMBO, WITH CHICKEN AND OYSTERS (Pensacola) (16)
(10 Servings)

Onions, lard, flour, salt and pepper
1 chicken (young hen) disjointed
1 pt. boiling water
50 oysters, with liquor
1 tbsp. prepared *filé*

Method:
1 Make roux (mixture) of onions, lard, flour, salt and pepper.
2 Place one chicken in the pot with roux.
3 Simmer gently until brown.
4 Add water.
5 Cook slowly until chicken is almost in pieces.
6 Half an hour before serving pour in oysters with their liquor.
7 Simmer for 5 minutes.
8 Immediately before serving, wet 1 tbsp. *filé* with the mixture.
9 Stir into pot until contents are slightly ropy.
10 Do not allow it to boil after the *filé* is added.
11 If not thick enough, add more *filé*.

DEVILED OYSTERS (11)
(6 Servings)

25 oysters, chopped fine
1 cup cracker crumbs
1 cup cream
1 tsp. mustard
1 tbsp. melted butter
½ tsp. salt
¼ tsp. pepper

Method:
1 Mix all ingredients.
2 Butter oyster shells or individual baking dishes.
3 Fill with mixture.
4 Bake about 20 minutes.
5 Serve immediately.

CREAMED OYSTERS IN RAMEKINS (1)
(6 Servings)

2½ tbsp. butter
3 tbsp. flour
¼ tsp. celery salt
½ tsp. salt
¼ tsp. white pepper
1 cup hot cream (thin)
1 pt. oysters
½ tsp. finely chopped parsley

Method:
1 Melt butter in a saucepan.
2 Add the flour mixed with seasonings.
3 Stir until well blended.
4 Add slowly hot cream and strained oyster liquor.
5 Stir until sauce is smooth.
6 Clean oysters.
7 Heat in their own liquor, until plump and edges curl.
8 Drain at once.
9 Re-heat in cream sauce.
10 Add parsley.
11 Turn into buttered ramekins.
12 Sprinkle with bread crumbs.
13 Brown in oven.

SCALLOPS

The edible portion of this shellfish, as prepared for market, is the adductor muscle. The meats vary in size from the small bay scallops ($\frac{3}{4}$-inch cubes) to the sea scallops (2 inches or more). If the larger scallops are used, split them across the grain to a thickness of about $\frac{1}{2}$ inch.

Scallop

BROILED SCALLOPS (15)
(6 Servings)

Scallops (1 qt.)
Fine bread crumbs
Beaten egg
Butter
Bacon strips
Mustard sauce

Method:

1 Wash scallops.
2 Drain thoroughly.
3 Dip in fine dry bread crumbs, beaten egg, and crumbs again.
4 Arrange on oven-proof plates.
5 Pour melted butter liberally over the scallops.
6 Arrange a strip of bacon across the plate.
7 Place under a broiler flame for 5 to 10 minutes, until the bacon is crisp and the scallops are tender.
8 Serve on the plates on which they are broiled with a mustard sauce.

Sauce

2 tbsp. dry mustard
Few drops of Worcestershire
sauce
2 tbsp. water
½ cup melted butter

Method:
1 Mix mustard and Worcestershire
sauce with 2 tbsp. water.
2 Add melted butter.

FRIED SCALLOPS (5)
(6 Servings)

1 qt. scallops
Salt solution
2 eggs
4 tbsp. water
Cracker or fine bread crumbs
Tartar sauce
Pepper

Method:
1 If scallops are large size, cut in
about ½ inch pieces.
2 Immerse for 3 minutes in salt solution (1 tbsp. salt to 1 cup cold
water).
3 Drain.
4 Dust with pepper
5 Beat eggs and add water.
6 Dip scallops in crumbs, egg, and
crumbs again.
7 Fry in deep fat at 360° F.
8 Serve with tartar sauce.

Suggestion: Scallops may be pan fried if preferred.

SCALLOPS WITH BACON (5)
(6 Servings)

1 qt. scallops
Bacon strips

Method:
1 Split large scallops to ½ inch in
size.
2 Boil in their own liquor until they
begin to shrink.
3 In baking dish place a layer of
bacon.
4 Cover with scallops.
5 Add top layer of bacon.
6 Bake at 375° F. until brown.

SAUTED SCALLOPS (5)
(6 Servings)

1 lb. scallops
1 small onion
2 tbsp. butter or bacon fat
Salt and pepper
Parsley, chopped
6 slices toast
Lemon

Method:
1 Cook scallops in a small amount of
water 5 minutes.
2 Drain.
3 Dry.
4 Cook minced onion in butter or
bacon fat until tender.
5 Add scallops.
6 Saute until brown.
7 Sprinkle with salt, pepper and
chopped parsley.
8 Serve on toast with lemon.

SEA SOUP (Scallops) (5)
(6 Servings)

2 cups scallops
1 tbsp. lemon juice
1 cup water
2 tbsp. butter
Salt and pepper to taste
1 qt. milk (hot)

Method:
1 Cut scallops very fine.
2 Sprinkle with lemon juice.
3 Cover and let stand 20 minutes.
4 Add water.
5 Slowly bring to boiling point.
6 Add butter, salt and pepper to taste.
7 Add milk.
8 Cook in double boiler 8 minutes.
9 May be strained before serving.

SCALLOP FRITTERS (5)
(6 Servings)

1 lb. scallops
Milk
2 Eggs
2 cups flour
1 tbsp. baking powder
½ tsp. salt
¼ tsp. pepper
1 tbsp. butter

Method:
1 Cook scallops in ¼ cup hot water or milk 5 minutes.
2 Drain.
3 Cut into small pieces.
4 Add enough milk to liquid drained from scallops to make 1 cup.
5 Pour into well beaten eggs.
6 Combine flour with baking powder, salt and pepper.
7 Stir liquid into flour mixture.
8 Beat hard.
9 Add butter, melted, and scallops.
10 Drop by spoonfuls into deep hot fat.
11 Fry golden brown.
12 Serve with cheese or other sauce.

DEVILED SCALLOPS (5)
(6 Servings)

Scallops
Sauce:
½ cup tomato sauce
1 tsp. prepared mustard
Juice of 1 lemon
½ tsp. salt
Cayenne

Method:
1 Cook scallops in small amount of water until they begin to shrivel.
2 Drain.
3 Simmer in sauce 2 minutes.
4 Serve on toast, topped with grated cheese.

SCALLOPS COCKTAIL (5)
(Individual)

5 scallops for each serving
Sauce

Method:
1 Cook scallops in small amount of water until they begin to shrivel.
2 Drain.
3 Chill.
4 If scallops are small, serve whole.
5 If large, cut in half.
6 Allow 5 small ones to a serving.
7 Place in cocktail glass.
8 Serve with any good sauce.

DONAX
(Coquina)

These tiny marine bi-valve mollusks, a little larger than a coffee bean, and of many colors, are found along all Florida beaches. As they are swept up by the surf, they immediately burrow and vanish into the wet sand. Occasionally vast quantities can be scooped up by hand in shallow pools. Usually, however, coquinas are collected by shoveling the sand into which they have disappeared into a mesh-bottomed box, and immersing the box into water to remove sand and debris. A peck will provide broth for half a dozen helpings.

To prepare: The coquinas must be thoroughly washed in cold fresh water. After washing, they are put into a kettle of hot water, filled just enough to cover the coquinas. The heat opens the shells and releases the juices. When the water comes to a boil, the operation is completed. Strain the broth through a fine cloth, season with a little salt and pepper. It can be drunk as bouillon, or by the addition of croutons, served as soup.

It is possible to keep the clear broth in a refrigerator for 24 hours, but it spoils easily, and is seldom found in markets.

COQUINA COCKTAIL

Coquina broth
Lemon juice
Tabasco sauce or other condiments

Method:
1 Chill coquina broth.
2 Add lemon juice, tabasco sauce, or other condiments.
3 Shake in cocktail shaker.
4 Serve immediately.

SHRIMP (2)
(30 Servings)

5 lbs. green shrimp
1 qt. water
2 cups celery, diced
3 slices lemon
3 tbsp. chopped onion
1 tbsp. whole black pepper
3½ tsp. salt

Method:
1 Bring water to a boil.
2 Add all ingredients except lemon.
3 Simmer 30 minutes while shrimp are being prepared.
4 Peel the shrimp by breaking the under shell from front of back. (This will allow the meat to be removed in one piece.)
5 Wash the shrimp in clear water.
6 Add lemon to kettle and boil 5 minutes.
7 Strain the liquid, discarding the solids.
8 Return the liquid to kettle and add water to bring the total up to about 3½ quarts.
9 Bring to a boil, add the shrimp, and boil for 5 to 10 minutes, or until shrimp are tender.
10 Remove the cooked shrimp and save the liquid for sauces, soups, etc.

SHRIMP A LA JACKSONVILLE (18)
(24 Servings)

4 lbs. whole shrimp
6 lemons (sliced)
¾ cup salt
3 tbsp. cayenne pepper

Method:
1 Plunge shrimp in kettle of boiling water, with lemons, salt and cayenne pepper.
2 Boil 20 minutes, and remove from kettle.
3 Remove heads and black vein, and shells.
4 Place in refrigerator to chill.
5 Use when desired in any of the following recipes.

Sauce

1 cup any good prepared mayonnaise
1 tbsp. tomato catsup
1 tsp. pepper
1 tbsp. horseradish
Juice of 1 lemon
¼ can condensed cream

Method:
1 Beat all together until the mixture thickens.
2 Serve cold.

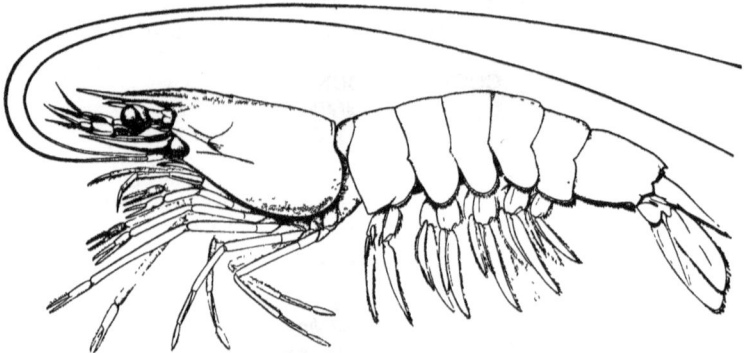

Shrimp

SHRIMP COCKTAIL (5)
(6 Servings)

1 lb. cooked shrimp
Cocktail sauce

Method:
1 Place cooked, cleaned shrimp in cocktail glasses.
2 Chill.
3 Use any desired cocktail sauce.

SHRIMP APPETIZER (4)
(Individual)

Sections of grapefruit
Whole, cooked shrimp
Mayonnaise

Method:
1 Arrange sections of grapefruit and whole shrimp in cocktail glass.
2 Cover with mayonnaise, or place in center 1 tbsp. mayonnaise mixed with tabasco sauce.

SHRIMP SALAD (5)
(6 Servings)

1 lb. cooked shrimp
2 cups finely minced celery
Juice of 1 lemon
½ tsp. salt
½ tsp. paprika
Mayonnaise to mix
Lettuce, shredded

Method:
1 Dice the shrimp.
2 Mix with celery, lemon juice, and seasoning.
3 Arrange in 6 nests shredded lettuce.
4 Use a small cup as a mold.
5 Fill with shrimp mixture and press firm.
6 Invert the molded contents into each lettuce nest.
7 Top with a tsp. of mayonnaise and paprika, or crossed strips of pimientos.

SHRIMP WIGGLE (5)
(6 Servings)

1 lb. cooked prepared shrimp
2 tbsp. butter (or oil)
2 medium sized onions
2 tbsp. flour
1 cup tomato soup
1 cup water
Crackers

Method:
1 Dice shrimp.
2 Fry onions in butter to golden brown.
3 Add flour.
4 When well mixed add tomato soup and water.
5 Stir constantly until thick.
6 Add shrimp.
7 Simmer 5 minutes.
8 Serve on toasted crackers.

FRENCH-FRIED SHRIMP
(6 Servings)

1½ lbs. green shrmp
Juice of 2 lemons
Salt and pepper
Cooking oil (or fat)
2 eggs well beaten
Sifted cracker crumbs

Method:
1 Peel the shrimp.
2 Wash and remove sand vein.
3 Place in a bowl with lemon juice, salt and pepper.
4 Allow to stand for 15 minutes.
5 Drain.
6 Heat cooking oil to 380° F.-400° F.
7 Dip shrimp in beaten egg and crumbs.
8 Place a single layer into a well oiled frying basket.
9 Cook for 3 minutes.
10 Drain on crushed paper.

CREOLE SHRIMP SALAD (4)
(8 Servings)

2 tbsp. granulated gelatin
4 tbsp. cold water
1 cup boiling water
1 cup fresh shrimp
1/3 cup chopped celery
½ cup chopped sweet pickles
½ tsp. salt
¼ tsp. pepper
1 cup canned tomato soup

Method:
1 Soak the gelatin in cold water for five minutes.
2 Add the boiling water.
3 Stir until gelatin is dissolved.
4 Cool.
5 Add remaining ingredients.
6 Pour into small molds which have been rinsed out with cold water.
7 Set in refrigerator to harden.
8 Unmold on lettuce.
9 Surround with mayonnaise.

SHRIMP-PINEAPPLE SALAD (4)
(8 Servings)

2 cups shrimp
½ cup vinegar
½ cup oil
Juice of 2 lemons
1 tsp. salt
1 tsp. white pepper
1 medium sized pineapple
Mayonnaise to mix

Method:
1 Mix shrimp, vinegar, oil, lemon juice, salt and white pepper.
2 Set in refrigerator for several hours.
3 Peel pineapple, and cut lengthwise in slender strips, about the size of shrimp.
4 Cover the pineapple with sugar.
5 Let stand while shrimp chill.
6 Drain shrimp.
7 Mix the pineapple and shrimp.
8 Cover with mayonnaise made from half pineapple juice and half lemon juice in place of vinegar usually called for.
9 Serve in lettuce cups.

BAKED SHRIMP WITH TOMATOES (4)
(12 Servings)

2 lbs. shrimp
2 tbsp. butter
2 cups canned tomatoes
Biscuit dough
Pepper, mace, nutmeg, and salt

Method:
1 Boil the shrimp.
2 Remove the shells.
3 Butter a deep dish.
4 Put in layer of biscuit dough.
5 Add layer of shrimp.
6 Dot with butter.
7 Add a layer of stewed tomatoes.
8 Add seasonings.
9 Repeat, using only two layers of biscuit dough.
10 Bake in hot oven (425° F.) for 45 minutes.
11 Serve hot.

Biscuit Dough

2 cups flour
4 tsp. baking powder
1 tsp. salt
2 tbsp. shortening
½ cup sweet milk

Method:
1 Sift together dry ingredients.
2 Cut in shortening.
3 Add the milk, and mix thoroughly.
4 Knead, and roll in thin layer on floured board.

Suggestion: Pounded biscuit may be used instead of biscuit dough.

CREAMED SHRIMP (4)
(4 Servings)

5 tbsp. butter
6 tbsp. flour
1 tsp. salt
½ tsp. paprika
¼ tsp. celery salt
2 tbsp. finely chopped parsley
2½ cups milk
1½ cups shrimp (cooked)

Method:
1 Melt the butter.
2 Add the flour, salt, paprika, celery salt, and parsley.
3 Add milk slowly.
4 Cook until smooth.
5 Stir constantly.
6 Add shrimp.
7 Heat through.
8 Serves four.

SHRIMP-STUFFED PEPPERS (4)
(6 Servings)

6 green peppers
1 tbsp. butter
1 cup mushrooms
½ tsp. minced onion
2 tbsp. minced tomatoes
1 cup cooked shrimp
1 tsp. salt
1 tsp. minced parsley
½ cup bread crumbs

Method:
1 Cut off tops of peppers, remove seeds.
2 Parboil peppers until tender.
3 Saute in butter the mushrooms, onions, tomato, and shrimp.
4 Add salt and parsley.
5 When all is heated together, dust in crumbs.
6 Fill peppers.
7 Place a piece of butter on each.
8 Bake 10 minutes in hot oven.

CURRIED SHRIMP (11)
(6 Servings)

1 cup shrimp (cooked)
1 cup boiled rice
3 tbsp. coconut
1 tbsp. curry powder
1 cup stock
1 tsp. salt

Method:
1 Mix all ingredients together, and put in baking dish.
2 Bake at 350° F. for 10 minutes.
3 Serve hot.

SHRIMP LOUISIANA (1)
(6 Servings)

1 tbsp. minced onion
4 tbsp. butter
2 tbsp. flour
1 cup rich milk
1½ cups cooked rice
1½ cups cooked and peeled shrimp
½ tsp. celery salt
1 tsp. salt
1 tsp. Worcestershire sauce
6 tbsp. canned tomato soup
¼ tsp. pepper

Method:
1 Cook onion in butter until golden brown.
2 Stir constantly.
3 Add flour, and milk.
4 Cook until smooth.
5 Add rice and shrimp.
6 When hot, add seasoning and tomato soup.

SHRIMP GUMBO (2)
(24 Servings)

1 cup shortening
5 tbsp. flour
1 large onion, sliced
1 clove garlic
1 lb. okra
5 cups water
4 lbs. cooked shrimp
Salt, parsley, bay leaves
Tabasco sauce

Method:
1 Heat shortening.
2 Stir in flour.
3 When brown, add onions, sliced; okra, chopped, and garlic.
4 Cook until soft.
5 Add the shrimp and water.
6 Let simmer slowly for three-quarters of an hour.
7 Add seasoning.
8 Before serving, add dash of Tabasco sauce.

SHRIMP PUDDING (5)
(6 Servings)

6 slices of bread, ¼ inch thick, buttered and cubed
1½ cups cooked shrimp
½ cup grated cheese
3 cups milk
3 eggs
1 tsp. salt
¼ tsp. paprika
⅛ tsp. pepper

Method:
1 Put half the bread cubes into a greased baking dish.
2 Add half the shrimp, and all the cheese.
3 Add remaining shrimp and bread cubes.
4 Mix milk, eggs, salt, paprika, and pepper.
5 Pour into baking dish.
6 Set dish in pan of hot water.
7 Bake in slow oven like custard.
8 It is done when knife comes out clean.

SHRIMPS—Oriental (5)
(6 Servings)

2 medium sized egg plants
4 slices bread, crumbed
1 small onion, minced
3 tbsp. tomato juice
1 cup shrimp, chopped
½ tsp. salt
¼ tsp. pepper
1 cup hot milk

Method:
1 Boil or bake egg plants until soft enough to scoop out pulp.
2 Chop pulp, add crumbs from slices of bread, onion, tomato juice, chopped shrimp, salt, pepper, and hot milk.
3 Pile mixture into eggplant shells or greased baking dish.
4 Top with crumbs.
5 Bake 30 minutes in moderate oven.

SHRIMP AND EGGS (5)
(6 Servings)

1 cup cooked shrimp
¼ cup finely diced celery
3 hard boiled eggs, sliced
6 stuffed olives
2 cups medium white sauce
¼ tsp. dry mustard

Method:
1 Mix all ingredients in saucepan.
2 Heat mixture slowly.
3 Serve on toast or with rice.

CUCUMBER BOATS (5)
(6 Servings)

6 cucumbers
½ cup mushrooms
2 tbsp. onion
3 tbsp. butter
1 cup shrimp
½ tbsp. parsley
2 tbsp. tomato juice
1 cup soft bread crumbs

Method:
1 Peel cucumbers.
2 Steam until soft enough to scoop out centers.
3 Save shell for stuffing.
4 Chop separately mushrooms, onions, shrimp, parsley, and cucumber pulp.
5 Saute mushrooms and onions in butter.
6 Add shrimp, parsley, tomato juice, and bread crumbs.
7 Season to taste.
8 Fill cucumber shells.
9 Top with buttered crumbs.
10 Bake at 400° F. until brown.

Suggestion: Use additional tomato juice if filling will not stick together.

SHRIMP—SPANISH STYLE (5)
(8 Servings)

½ cup green pepper
2 cups shrimp
1 medium onion
1½ cups cooked rice
½ cup mushrooms
2 cups tomatoes
Salt and pepper
2 tbsp. oil

Method:
1 Chop pepper, onion, shrimp and mushrooms.
2 Saute green peppers and onion in oil until soft.
3 Add shrimp, rice, mushrooms, tomatoes, salt and pepper.
4 Mix well.
5 Cover.
6 Cook slowly 10 minutes.
7 Or cover with crumbs and bake until top browns.

SHRIMP SANDWICH FILLING (5)
(4 Servings)

1 cup cooked shrimp
2 tbsp. celery
½ tsp. onion juice
Salt and pepper
Mayonnaise

Method:
1 Chop shrimp fine.
2 Add finely chopped celery and onion juice.
3 Season to taste with salt and pepper.
4 Add enough mayonnaise to make a spreadable paste.

SPANISH SHRIMP PILAU (11)
(12 Servings)

2 lbs. green shrimp
1/3 lb. salt pork, diced
4 medium sized onions, sliced
1 small green pepper, or red sweet
  pepper
1 small can tomatoes
1 small-datil pepper (very hot)
3½ cups water
2 cups best rice
1 tbsp. salt

Method:

1 Clean shrimp by removing shell and sand vein.
2 Wash.
3 Cut in two.
4 Chop bacon, onions and peppers.
5 Fry these three together in large heavy pot until light brown.
6 Add tomatoes, shrimp and water.
7 When mixture boils add rice and salt.
8 Cook slowly 20 minutes.
9 Rice grains should be separate.

Suggestion: Thyme and other herbs may be added.

CREOLE SHRIMP JAMBALAYA (6)
(15 Servings)

2 cups (onions
      (green peppers
      (ham
      (celery
1 clove garlic
4 tbsp. butter or olive oil
4 cups water
1 lb. rice
2 lbs. green shrimp
2 cups tomatoes
½ tsp. spanish saffron
½ tbsp. salt

Method:

1 Chop onions, green peppers, ham, celery and garlic.
2 Saute in butter or oil.
3 Add water.
4 When mixture boils, add rice.
5 Clean shrimp by removing shell and sand vein and washing.
6 Add shrimp to boiling mixture.
7 Add tomatoes, saffron and salt.
8 Bring to boil again.
9 Cover tightly, place in oven.
10 Cook at 350° F. from 20 to 25 minutes.
11 Serve with tomato sauce and grated cheese.

CURRIED SHRIMPS A L'INDIENNE (6)
(12 Servings)

1 tbsp. grated coconut
¼ cup milk
1 cup onion
1 clove garlic
1 apple
2 tbsp. butter
1 tbsp. curry powder
1 tbsp. flour
1 qt. stock
1 tbsp. Bengal Chutney
1 large tomato, chopped
2 lbs. shrimp
4 tbsp. butter
  Boiled rice

Method:

1 Soak cocoanut in milk.
2 Chop onion, garlic and apple.
3 Saute in butter until light brown.
4 Add curry powder, flour, stock, Chutney, tomato and cocoanut with milk.
5 Simmer until consistency of cream sauce.
6 Brown shrimp in butter.
7 Add to sauce.
8 Heat 5 minutes.
9 Serve with boiled rice.

SEA MUSSELS

Sea mussels, larger than the fresh-water variety, are similar to clams. They are found in quantities along the Florida coasts, and in the broad estuaries of its many rivers.

Mussels have blue-black shells, which should be tightly closed when caught or purchased, showing they are alive. They are steamed open, or opened with a sharp knife, care being taken not to cut the meat. When open, immediately remove the black tuft, known as "beard."

Prepare and serve the same as clams.

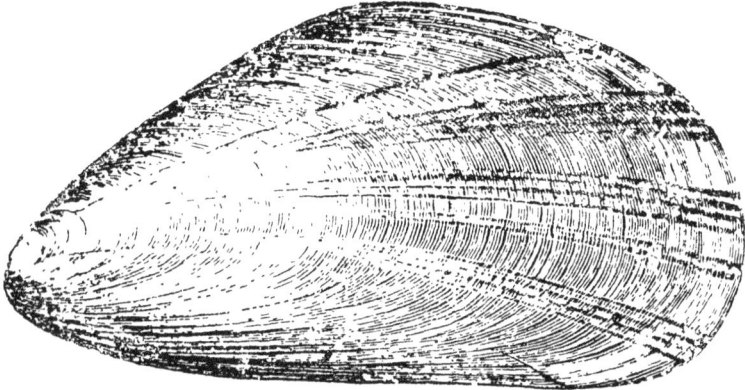

Sea Mussel

TURTLE

The turtles found in Florida are the common alligator snapper, the loggerhead and the mud turtle. Green and log-

Green Turtle

gerhead turtles are captured in large nets for the market. In Key West are "turtle crawls"—fenced-in corrals or pens extending out into the water—where turtles are confined alive awaiting shipments to various markets, or preparatory to being butchered for conversion into soup and canned meat.

TURTLE STEAKS

Turtle steaks may be purchased in South Florida fish markets. If small, the steaks are dredged in flour and fried the same as any other meat. If large, fry until a golden brown, then cover with water, and cook over a slow fire until tender.

Variations:
1. Serve with tomato sauce.
2. Add rich cream sauce and serve same as chicken.
3. A can of peas, ½ cup mushrooms, ½ cup celery may be added to meat when it is tender

TURTLE SOUP (10)
(2 cups—6 Servings)

Turtle meat
6 medium potatoes, diced
5 small onions, chopped
1 small can evaporated milk
Salt and pepper

Method:
1 Cut turtle meat in small pieces.
2 Place in a heavy cooking pot.
3 Cover with water.
4 Cook until meat is tender.
5 Add potatoes and onions.
6 Cook until meat and vegetables are done.
7 A little canned cream may be added just before serving.
8 Season to taste.

TURTLE CROQUETTES (14)
(2 Cups—6 Servings)

Leftover turtle meat
Beaten egg
Bread crumbs
Cracker meal
Fat

Method:
1 Grind leftover baked turtle meat.
2 Mix with egg and bread crumbs.
3 Mold into cones or cakes.
4 Dip in beaten egg.
5 Roll in cracker meal.
6 Fry in deep fat.
7 Drain on crushed paper.

TURTLE LOAF (7)
(6 Servings)

3 cups baked leftover turtle meat
1 cup bread crumbs
2 eggs
Salt and pepper
1 cup stock (liquid in which turtle has been cooked)

Method:
1 Grind turtle meat.
2 Mix with bread crumbs.
3 Season with salt and pepper.
4 Mold in rounded loaf.
5 Pour over 1 cup stock.
6 Garnish with pimientos in strips.
7 Place in oven until browned on top.
8 Serve with rice to which saffron has been added while cooking.

KEY WEST TURTLE STEW

2 lbs. turtle meat (with fat)
2 qts. hot water
2 medium onions, chopped
3 tbsp. bacon fat
1 can tomato puree
2 large potatoes, diced
2 tsp. salt
⅛ tsp. pepper

Method:

1 Cut turtle meat into small cubes
2 Cover with hot water.
3 Cook 15 minutes.
4 Drain, reserve stock.
5 Saute onions in fat until light brown.
6 Add turtle meat.
7 Saute until brown on all sides.
8 Add hot stock.
9 Simmer until tender.
10 Add tomato, potato, salt and pepper.
11 Cook 20 minutes.
12 Serve very hot with crackers or pilot biscuits.

TERRAPIN

A species of land tortoise, this terrapin is known as the "Florida Gopher."

GOPHER STEW (17)

Thick meat of the back of gopher
3 medium potatoes
2 small onions
  Water to cover
  Salt and pepper
  Cayenne

Method:

1 Wash gopher.
2 Cook in boiling water until shell is easily removed.
3 Use only thick meat of back attached to upper shell.
4 Chop meat, potatoes and onions.
5 Place in a kettle.
6 Cover with water.
7 Season to taste.
8 Simmer until tender.

GOPHER STEAKS (17)

(6 to 8 Servings according to size)

Gopher meat sliced thick
Flour
Fat

Method:

1 Boil gopher in water until shell can be removed.
2 Slice meat into steaks.
3 Roll in flour.
4 Cook in hot fat over slow fire until tender.

HOME CANNING

A variety of canned meats and vegetables in the pantry, supplemented by a supply of Florida's low-cost seafoods, is not only a household economy, but no small item in local citizens' participation in the National Defense Program.

Detailed information on home canning is treated in Bulletin No. 87, issued by the State Home Demonstration Department, Tallahassee, Florida, and Farmers' Bulletin No. 1762, issued by the U. S. Department of Agriculture, Washington, D. C. Both may be obtained free upon request.

A steam-pressure cooker is absolutely necessary to the satisfactory canning of seafoods. Authorities recommend the use of tin, not glass, containers. There are many home can sealers on the market. Home demonstration agents are available in nearly all Florida counties to instruct those unfamiliar with canning processes. In many cases the agents provide the necessary equipment and supervise the work.

General Directions

In a bulletin entitled **Home Cannery of Fishery Products** Isabelle S. Thursby, Extension Economist, Florida State College for Women, issued the following instructions:

Do not attempt to can fish unless absolutely sure they are fresh. As soon as caught, it is well to kill them immediately with a knife and let the blood run out. (This is made easier by dipping fish in boiling water. If skin is very tough, remove this also, and wash the fish in clear water. Remove entrails and the dark membrane found in some fish, as in mullet, covering the abdominal cavity. In small fish, the backbone may be left in. In the larger fishes, remove the backbone, and use with what meat adheres to it in chowders.

It is well, in order to draw out all the blood before canning, to place the fish in brines strong enough to float a potato. (Vary time according to thickness of fish, from a few minutes to an hour).

FISH CHOWDER

Method:

Fish scraps (heads and backbones)
Cold water to cover
3 medium onions
3 medium potatoes
Salt and pepper to taste
Milk

1 Cover fish scraps with cold water.
2 Simmer until meat slips from bones.
3 Remove from stock.
4 Pick meat from bones.
5 To the stock, add chopped onions and diced potatoes.
6 Simmer until vegetables are almost done.
7 Season to taste.
8 Pack in hot cans.
9 Process immediately.
10 When ready to serve, add 1 qt. of milk.
11 Serve hot with crackers.

CANNED FISH

Method:

Fish
Heavy brine solution
Salt

1 Remove the fish from the brine.
2 Drain well.
3 Cut in can lengths.
4 Dip quickly into boiling water to shrink.
5 Pack closely in can to within ½ inch of top.
6 Add ½ tsp. salt.
7 Seal while hot.
8 Process.
9 Cool immediately.

FISH ROE A LA SPENCER

Method:

Fish roe
Salted water
Salted milk
Bread crumbs, sifted.
Cooking oil

1 Select clean fish roe with skin unbroken.
2 If there is any small opening in the skin, tie it with a piece of thread.
3 Wash in salted water.
4 Pat dry with a coarse towel.
5 Dip each piece of roe into heavily salted milk, then into finely sifted bread crumbs.
6 Oil a baking pan.
7 Place the roe in it.
8 Sprinkle liberally over the top with oil.
9 Bake in very hot oven (550° F.) for 10 to 15 minutes according to the thickness of roe.
10 Pack immediately while hot.
11 Seal and process No. 2 tins 50 minutes at 15 pounds pressure.

SHRIMP (20)

Shrimp should be used when absolutely fresh—at the shore, if possible—as they deteriorate quickly. They may be peeled or left unshelled until cooked. Either way they are boiled in salted water, 1 lb. salt to 1 gallon of water. Shrimp should be packed into inside-lacquered cans.

Shrimp
Weak brine

Method—Wet Pack:

1 Boil shrimp 5 minutes.
2 Peel.
3 Pack in cans.
4 Fill in with a weak brine (1 tbsp. salt to 1 qt. boiling water) to within ½ inch of top.
5 Process 30 minutes at 10 pounds pressure.

Method—Dry Pack:

1 Boil shrimp 5 minutes.
2 Peel.
3 Pack dry into cans adding no liquid.
4 Process 30 minutes at 15 pounds pressure.

Suggestion: In case inside-lacquered cans cannot be had, the shrimp may be put into ordinary tin cans lined with parchment paper at sides, bottom, and top. They may also be put in small glass jars.

OYSTERS (20)

In canning oysters, care must be taken to see that they are absolutely fresh, have not "soured," and contain no oysters that are spoiled.

Oysters
Brine
¼ pound of salt to 5 quarts of water

Method:

1 Best results are to open the oysters by hand.
2 Reject those where the shell is partly open, which indicates this particular oyster is dead.
3 Rinse the oysters to be sure that no particles of shell or grit are put into the cans.
4 Pack 16 ounces of oyster meat into a No. 2 can and fill with boiling brine—¼ pound of salt to 5 quarts of water.
5 Fill to within ½ inch of top of can.
6 Exhaust 10 minutes at 212° F.
7 This may be done by placing the cans in steam pressure, with water boiling in bottom of retort.
8 Keep it boiling, put on the lid, but leave the petcock open to allow the steam to escape.
9 Seal and process 30 minutes at 15 pounds pressure.

SPICED FISH (20)

Fish, (mackerel, sea trout, or mullet
Brine (½ lb. salt to one gal. water)

Method:

1 Scrape off all scales and slime.
2 Clean and wash thoroughly, remove all waste material and inner black membrane in mullet.
3 Split the fish in two pieces but do not remove backbone.
4 Cut the cleaned fish into can-length pieces.
5 Soak in brine for one hour.
6 Drain for 10 minutes.
7 Place in containers, fish averaging 20 ounces, packed rather loosely.
8 Fill cans with vinegar sauce.
9 About 27 lbs. of fish will be required to fill a dozen No. 2 cans or pint jars.

Spiced Vinegar Sauce (20)

¼ oz. whole white pepper
⅛ oz. bay leaves
½ oz. whole cloves
¼ oz. mustard seed
⅛ oz. cracked cardemon seed
⅛ oz. cracked whole ginger
2 qts. vinegar
1 pt. water
2 oz. sugar

Method:

1 Tie all spices in a bag.
2 Add to remaining ingredients.
3 Simmer 1 hour.
4 Strain before using.

Process:

1 Place jars or tins in cold water 2 inches below rims.
2 Boil 20 minutes.
3 Insert on wire rack to drain.
4 In each container place 2 slices raw onion, 1 bay leaf, 1 tsp. mixed spices, 1 tbsp. olive oil.
5 Add fish.
6 Cover with spiced vinegar.
7 Seal pint jars loosely.
8 Process: 1½ hours, 10 pound pres· sure at 240° F.
9 For tins, clinch lids loosely.
10 Steam 10 minutes at 212° F.
11 Seal cans immediately.
12 Process for 80 minutes at 10 lbs. pressure 240° F.
13 Cool any containers in cooker, before removing.

MACKEREL IN TOMATO SAUCE (20)

About 33 lbs. fish
1 doz. No. 2 cans or pint jars

Method:

1 Fill the jars with the hot tomato sauce to within ½ inch of rim.
2 Seal immediately.
3 Process for 100 minutes at 10 pounds pressure, 240° F.
4 Release pressure slowly.
5 If pack is made in tin, pack with fish, and fill with hot sauce.
6 Seal immediately.
7 Process for 90 minutes at 10 pounds pressure.
8 About 33 lbs. of fish will be required to fill a dozen No. 2 cans or pint jars.

Tomato Sauce (20)
Method:

1 gal. tomato puree
6 tbsp. spiced vinegar sauce
½ oz. ground horseradish
2 tbsp. minced onion
1 oz. salt

1 Mix the ingredients.
2 Boil down to one-half the original volume.

SMOKED MULLET (7)
Take fresh mullet in season, clean carefully, and split down back. (Heads, tails, and fins may be left on). Salt over night, or at least for 2 hours. Wash again in clean water and allow to drip. When dry hang in smokehouse. This is usually made of sheet tin 3 feet square and 5 feet in height, with a 2-hole draft with knob, at bottom of entrance door, and a series of circular holes at ceiling level on opposite side to afford proper draft and escape for smoke. Wooden racks extend from side to side of smokehouse, with nails at close intervals, which are thrust through mullet heads.

The fire, preferably of hickory wood, which gives the best flavor, is started on the floor, then smothered with sawdust to insure plenty of smoke. The mullet should be smoked from two to 10 hours. (NOTE: Oak wood burns too fast, and pine makes too much smoke or soot.)

SALT WATER MULLET (7)
Mullet caught in salt water may be smoked immediately over an out-of-door furnace, grill, or barbecue pit, after being properly cleaned and washed in sea water which gives sufficient seasoning. The fat of the mullet prevents burning and imparts a delicious flavor.

QUANTITY SERVINGS (6)

Parties, picnics, political gatherings, lodge and church suppers form an important part of Florida public life. To assist cooks in the preparation of quantity servings, the following advice and recipes were furnished by Clark Bowdish, steward of the San Carlos Hotel, Pensacola.

Clams should be purchased by the hundred or barrel. You can tell the bad ones by the odor. If the shell is open, the clam is probably dead and should be thrown out. A quick method to determine whether a clam is dead or not, is to dump a bushel or more into fresh water. The dead ones rise to the surface.

A good shell-fish man will not have to wash off clams or oysters after opening. Washing ruins the taste of shellfish. They must be left in their own juice to retain their full flavor. In serving on the half shell, arrange with hinge towards center, with cocktail sauce in glass server in center.

Before steaming clams, rinse off in fresh water. Soft clams dug out of sand are apt to be gritty, so it is better to dump them into salt water until they have drunk in water and expelled the sand. Put in pot with very little water, cover and boil. The steam cooks them. When pot boils up to top and clams are opened slightly, they are done. The liquor that has been steamed out is the broth which is served in a cup with the clams. Drawn butter, or a hot sauce made of milk, flour, black pepper, vinegar and a little chopped parsley, is also served.

Good crab meat has a fresh sea smell. Frozen meat has little or no odor. Claw meat is tastiest, but is not used for cocktails because of its dark color. It is fine for gumbos and au gratin dishes. Back fin is the best, but expensive and scarce.

Maine lobster is shipped alive in ice and seaweed. Upon receipt, uncrate immediately and cull out dead ones. Cook at once and use for salads. For broiling, split and salt the meat. Sprinkle generously with paprika. If this is not used, meat will look gray. Butter and broil.

RED SNAPPER CHOWDER
(100 Portions)

10 lb. red snapper
4 gal. water
2 lbs. chopped onions
3 lbs. diced green peppers
1½ No. 10 canned tomatoes
½ lb. diced bacon
½ gal. diced potatoes
1 clove garlic
1 tbsp. paprika
Dash red pepper or Cayenne
Salt and pepper

Method:

1 Dice fish in about 1 in. squares.
2 Boil fish with a few heads and water until fish is about half done.
3 Leave fish in stock thus made.
4 Add: onions, green peppers, canned tomatoes, garlic, pepper or cayenne, paprika, salt and pepper to taste.
5 Add bacon, and potatoes.
6 *Do not thicken.*
7 If necessary, add more tomatoes and potatoes.
8 Dry sherry, a few bay leaves, a few peppercorns and thyme add to flavor.

LOBSTER BISQUE
Use same recipe as for crawfish, substituting lobster.

DEVILED CRABS
(30 Portions)

1½ oz. onions, chopped
2 oz. butter ⎫
2 oz. flour ⎬ Cream sauce
2 cups milk ⎭
2 eggs
4 lbs. crab meat
2 tbsp. Worcestershire sauce
4 tbsp. parsley, chopped
½ tsp. red pepper
2 tbsp. salt
Bread crumbs

Method:

1 Add onion to prepared cream sauce and cook, but do not brown.
2 Soak bread in milk, squeeze out.
3 Add to mixture, together with crab meat and beaten egg.
4 Season to taste.
5 Mix well and fill shells.
6 Dip in egg, flour, and bread crumbs.
7 Fry in deep fat.
8 Serve one portion with tartar sauce, French fried potatoes and coleslaw.

Sheepshead

CLAM CHOWDER
(8 Gallons)

75 large open clams
5 gal. fish stock
3 qts. diced potatoes
1 qt. diced onions
2 tbsp. thyme
1 qt. diced celery
1 qt. diced carrots
1½ No. 10 canned tomatoes
Small amount of sugar
Salt and pepper

Method:
1 Rinse clams in cold water.
2 Place in large kettle with small amount of water.
3 Allow to come to a boil.
4 Remove from heat.
5 Skim and save the liquid.
6 Chop or mince clams fine.
7 Cook vegetables in stock until tender.
8 Mix vegetables and clams.
9 Serve hot.

CRAWFISH BISQUE (6)
(36 Portions)

3 doz. crawfish
1 large onion
1 carrot
1 bay leaf
Sprig of parsley
6 whole cloves
2 cloves garlic
Thyme
Butter
1 gal. fish bouillon
1 cup raw rice
1 glass brandy (optional)
1 glass white wine (optional)
Stuffing:
1 fried chopped onion
½ clove garlic
Parsley
Meat of crawfish, chopped fine
Bread (squeezed)
Milk
1 egg
Seasoning

Method:
1 Soak crawfish in water overnight
2 Remove tails.
3 Pick out meat.
4 Empty heads and save for stuffing.
5 Take all shells and insides of heads and chop or grind very fine.
6 Chop onion and carrot very fine.
7 Fry onion, carrot, bay leaf, parsley, cloves, garlic, and a little thyme in butter.
8 Add chopped shells and insides of heads and fry again.
9 To this add bouillon and rice and cook slowly 1 hour.
10 Strain through sieve and season to taste.
11 If available, add one small glass of brandy before putting in bouillon, light it and extinguish with glass of white wine.
12 While soup is cooking, make the stuffing.
13 Stuff heads with this and bake or broil.
14 Add to soup when serving.

CREAM OF OYSTER SOUP

(10 Gallons)
2 gal. oysters (standards)
3 qts. water
4 lbs. butter
2 lbs. flour
8 gal. milk
¾ cup salt
(15 Gallons)
3 gal. oysters (standards)
4½ qts. water
6 lbs. butter
3 lbs. flour
12 gal. milk
1⅛ cup salt

Method:
1 Cook oysters in water for 5 min.
2 Lift oysters from water, strain oyster juice through a fine sieve.
3 Make cream sauce of remaining ingredients.
4 Chop oysters into about ½-inch pieces.
5 Add oysters and broth to cream sauce.
6 Season.
7 Do not overcook oysters.
8 Plenty of butter is needed to bring out real flavor of oysters.

ESCALLOPED OYSTERS
(50 Portions)

1 gal. oysters
1 gal. crackers (broken)
1¼ lb. butter
2 tbsp. salt
1 tbsp. celery salt
½ tsp. pepper

Method:

1 Clean oysters.
2 Place layer of oysters in a steam-table pan or baking dish.
3 Sprinkle with salt, celery salt, and pepper.
4 Mix crackers and melted butter.
5 Cover lightly with crackers.
6 Repeat with oysters, seasoning, and crackers.
7 (Make only 2 layers).
8 Bake 30 to 35 minutes in oven heated to 375° F.

REMOULADE SAUCE
(Three Quarts)

2 bunches green onions
1 cup celery, diced
3 cloves garlic
1 cup Tarragon vinegar
4 egg yolks, hard boiled
½ cup capers
1 cup mixed sweet pickles
1 cup sour onions, pickled
4 tbsp. Creole mustard
1 cup tomato catsup
½ cup paprika
1 qt. mayonnaise

Method:

1 Chop fine the green onions, celery, and garlic.
2 Simmer in the Tarragon vinegar until done.
3 Strain through fine sieve.
4 Add the yolks of the hard-boiled eggs.
5 Chop capers, pickles, and pickled onions.
6 Blend all ingredients into the mayonnaise.

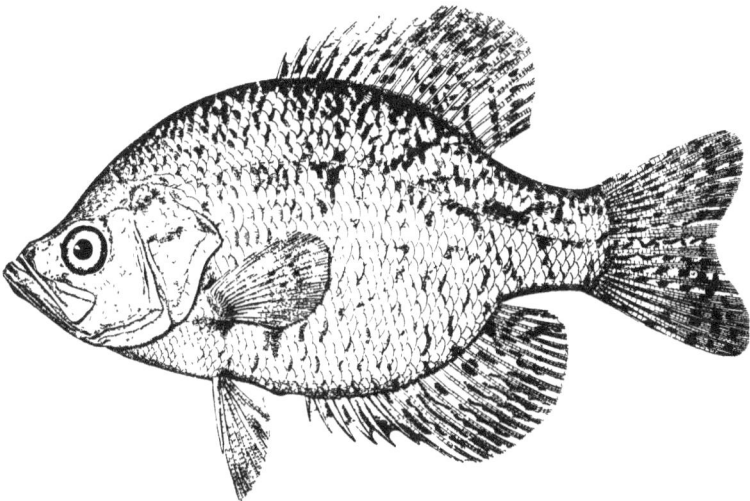

Black Crappie

CITATIONS

(1) Jackson, Josephine — *Sunshine Cook Book*

(2) U. S. Department of Commerce — *Practical Fish Cookery*—Fishery Circular No. 19

(3) Corse, Herbert M. — Jacksonville, Florida

(4) Sarasota Woman's Club — *Florida Cook Book*

(5) Atlantic Coast Fisheries Co. — *Nordic Seafoods* (Permission given to use)

(6) Bowdish, Clark, Caterer — San Carlos Hotel, Pensacola, Florida (Permission given to use)

(7) Shepherd, Miss Rose — WPA Florida Writers Project

(8) Knowles, Mrs. Laura — Key West, Florida

(9) Woman's Club of Jacksonville — *Woman's Club Cook Book* (Permission given to use)

(10) Key West *Citizen* — "Prize Winning Recipes," March 2, 1938

(11) Apalachicola *Times* — "Prize Winning Recipes," November 2, 1935

(12) Evangeline Pepper & Food Products Co. St. Martinsville, Louisiana — *Creole Cooking Recipes*

(13) Miami *Daily News* — "Prize Recipes" August 12, 1941

(14) DeWitt, Bernard, Volunteer Consultant — Tampa, Florida

(15) Meredith Publishing Co. Des Moines, Iowa — *Better Homes and Gardens Cook Book*

(16) Hargis, Modeste — *Unusual Dishes in West Florida* Pensacola, Florida

(17) U. S. I.—Florida Section — Florida WPA Writers' Project, 1940

(18) DuBose, Mrs. Mazelle — WPA Florida Writers' Project

(19) *St. Augustine Shrimp Fleet* School Reader — WPA Florida Writers' Project

96 INDEX

www.ingramcontent.com/pod-product-compliance
Lightning Source LLC
Chambersburg PA
CBHW021344090426
42742CB00008B/741